MW01155145

Change Does Not Occur in A Flash

Change Does Not Occur in A Flash

To Gary,
Thanks for pushing you
to attend the University
of Notre Dame. I changed
the landscape of our
school!
Blessings to you!
Flash

Darrell Gordon

Gordon
#38

Library of Congress Control Number: 2018909313

ISBN: Hardcover 978-1-9845-4556-5
Softcover 978-1-9845-4555-8
eBook 978-1-9845-4554-1

Print information available on the last page.

Rev. date: 08/06/2018

To order additional copies of this book, contact:
Xlibris
1-888-795-4274
www.Xlibris.com
Orders@Xlibris.com
773280

CONTENTS

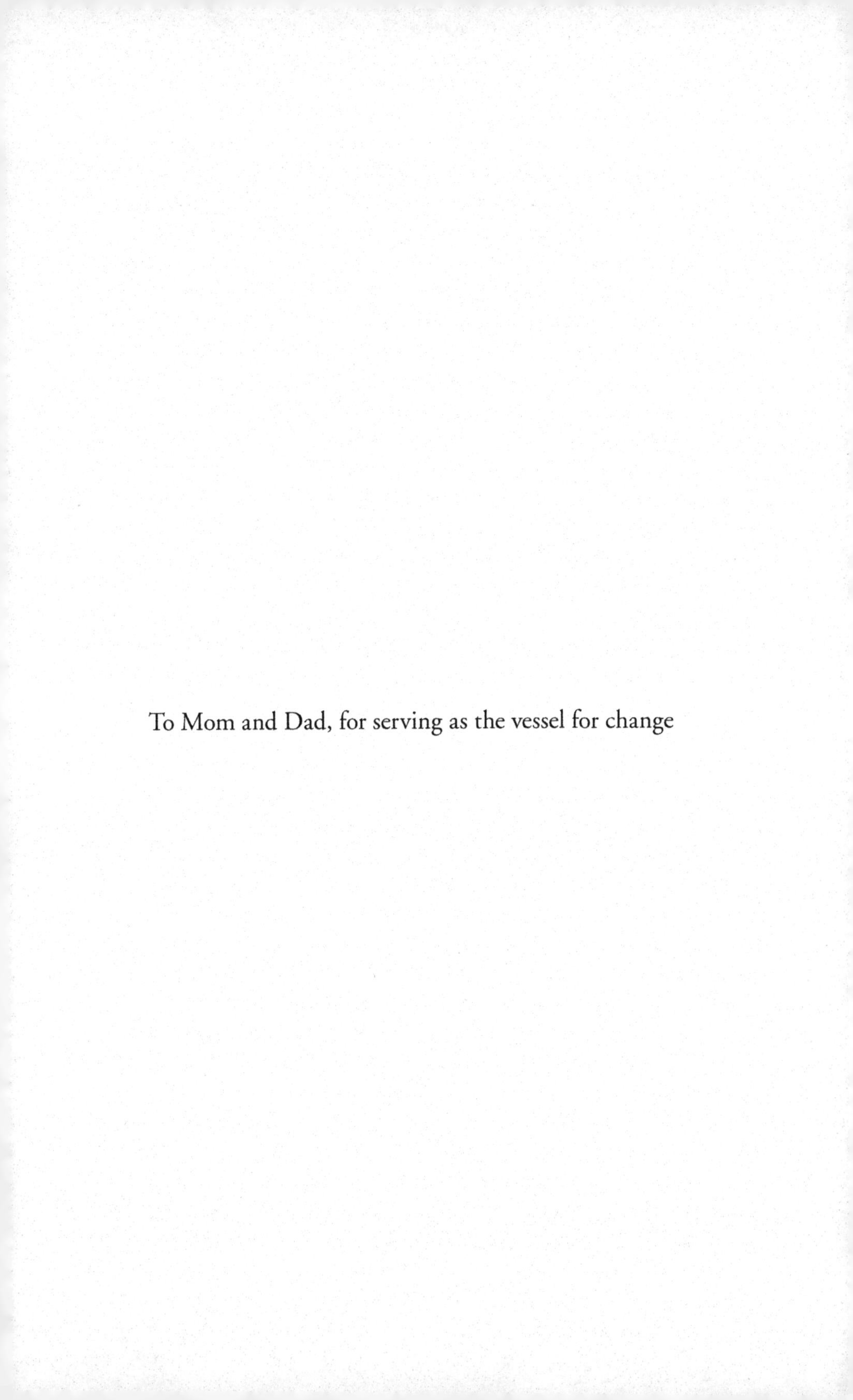

To Mom and Dad, for serving as the vessel for change

FOREWORD

ANYONE WHO'S EVER met me knows I'm a huge Notre Dame fan. I graduated from the university back in 1953 with a degree in sociology. I am still the football team's number one fan.

Coaching legends like Frank Leahy, Ara Parseghian, and Lou Holtz often meant more to the student body than the actual teachers themselves. They taught us more about being good students and how important it was to take advantage of our education. Even in my later years, I can appreciate what they were teaching me. I'm the beneficiary of a lot of amazing things that I learned at Notre Dame.

I'll never forget when Darrell "Flash" Gordon and his teammates clenched the national championship in 1988. It was such a proud moment for Fighting Irish fans everywhere. Since that moment, Darrell has demonstrated his strength of character on and off the field, motivating everyone he comes into contact with.

Darrell is a great guy. And if you follow his FLASH points, he will lead you to greatness too.

Regis Philbin
Class of 1953

INTRODUCTION

NOTRE DAME FOOTBALL players squeeze through a tight doorway stairwell as they take steps toward history at every home game. Some are relaxed. Some are hyper. Some are praying. Some are so nervous they've spent the last half hour being sick in the bathroom.

All are glittering gladiators, dressed for battle in uniforms and helmets that have been freshly painted with flecks of gold dust. Their cleats scrape the cement steps as their taped hands reach up to slap a simple sign that reads Play Like a Champion Today.

They alight one by one through a nondescript door into a sloping tunnel that is also shared with opponents. Family, friends, and Notre Dame faithfuls reach out and touch the Irish gladiators as they clop-clop down toward the bright light at the end of the tunnel.

The players nervously stomp their feet, punch one another, and build their voices as they gather just outside of view and await the word to charge onto the historic grass field and hear the roar of eighty thousand people.

They will gather strength from the support as they face the moment-by-moment transformations that make up a game. They will gather strength from higher places. The famed Golden Dome and the outstretched arms of Touchdown Jesus have got their backs. So do the fans on hand and tens of millions more who are connected through their televisions, radios, and computer screens.

Here's what Lou Holtz, my coach and friend, told a pregame rally in 2008 about what comes to his mind when you say Notre Dame: "It's about God, it's about our blessed lady on the dome, it's about faith, it's about support, it's about never giving up no matter what the odds are, WE ARE NOTRE DAME AND WE ARE SPECIAL!"

Moments are truly golden before Notre Dame's home football games. The results that follow are paved in gold too. Hundreds of victories and a record eleven national championships prove that.

I played on the last championship team, in 1988. Fans can sense more championships coming on the horizon. Notre Dame came close under Coach Brian Kelly, with a perfect record going into the title game for the 2012 season.

These players are no different than anyone else on this campus in every respect, except one on game days. They are prepared for battle and no longer recognizable to their classmates, family, and friends. They've changed in dress and demeanor. They are possessed with carrying on a winning tradition. They are modern-day gladiators playing in an old-fashioned stadium.

The tunnel entrance is the same one where Miami and Notre Dame players pushed and shoved before the "Game of the Century" that essentially decided the 1988 national championship. The Irish were inspired to win that game in large part when Holtz shocked his players by not scolding them after the fracas. In fact, he fired us into a frenzy by saying that nobody should get near Miami coach Jimmy Johnson if another scrap should break out. "I'll kick his a——," Holtz told us.

The players roared, and the tension was gone. We knew victory would be ours that day, inspired by a speech that was just as important to us as the infamous "Win One for the Gipper" by legendary coach Knute Rockne.

We played like champions. Some traditions never change. But some do because they have to. College teams can't win without adjusting to the times. Holtz knew when he arrived that he needed faster, stronger players to compete regularly with the Miamis, the Michigans, and the USCs. He knew Notre Dame needed better practice facilities, and it needed better tutors because many of the players he needed didn't come from strong academic backgrounds.

Change is happening every year. Coach Kelly is facing big challenges as he seeks the top again. To compete for championships, he knows Notre Dame needs to step up in recruiting, in coaching, in executing plays, and in adding FieldTurf and Jumbotrons. Notre Dame needs to play like a champion to be a champion. But that's no different than real life.

People must adjust to every up and down in their lives, whether they are football players or firefighters, CEOs or secretaries, pastors or painters. I am here to tell you that no matter what your circumstances, you *can* transform yourself. You can walk through a tunnel of darkness and find the light. You can live like a champion today.

Yes, this book is an autobiography, but it's more than that. It is about making profound changes that can take your life from ordinary to extraordinary. It's about living with character, commitment, and Christian spirit. It's about loving and laughing a lot too.

Life should be outstanding. I believe that mine is. Yours can be too.

All the ideas and the advice in this book are gathered from my personal experiences and are designed to help people overcome obstacles to change. (They helped me develop a five-step foundation for major changes that I call FLASH points. The essential step is establishing support systems.) I want to inspire you. I want to convince you to take steps forward—to make the changes that you truly want and need.

This is my life story. It is also a story of foundations laid by great leaders, great parents, and great campuses. They are driving forces in change. We all need mentors who model greatness, whether they are parents, siblings, teachers, preachers, politicians, coaches, or any other leaders.

God granted me athletic gifts. He gave me the gifts of speed and strength that helped me acquire the nickname Flash, which was bestowed on me as a youngster in my Pop Warner football days. Those gifts allowed me to succeed in ways that most others could not. They placed me on the 1988 national championship team for Notre Dame.

God also granted me the gift of perseverance, which I needed in huge doses to adjust to the academic rigors and other obstacles I faced while I played for the Irish. You might say that Notre Dame stretched my mind like Silly Putty. I had to change, to stretch my whole being, and just to survive and thrive there.

Notre Dame exposed an institutional model that promotes leadership and stewardship. My experience there bestowed on me so much more than two degrees and the chance to play on a national championship team. It deepened my spirituality, introduced me to a more diverse group of friends who have gone on to have a great impact on society, took me to the White House to visit with two presidents, and landed me an internship on Wall Street. It made me a better father, a better CEO, and a better man.

Campuses mold and enthuse people. They help cultivate the relationships that drive students to achieve and to change throughout their lives. I have been the beneficiary of four great campuses. Those are Hillside High School in New Jersey, the University of Notre Dame, Chase College of Law at Northern Kentucky, and Wernle Youth & Family Treatment Center. I earned degrees at the first three, and I have been constantly learning and changing while serving as CEO at Wernle for seventeen years.

Wernle Youth & Family Treatment Center is a facility that treats boys and girls who have been abused, abandoned, and neglected. It's a family-focused, child-centered agency that provides opportunities for the growth, development, and treatment of troubled children and their families—individually, interpersonally, and socially—through best-practice programs and a variety of therapy approaches. Our core purpose is "rebuilding relationships and restoring hope." Wernle has exploded with growth in the last few years, something that happened because of change, because of a focus on positive outcomes, financial success, and long-term sustainability.

Together, campuses have enveloped me for far more than half of my life. There's no doubt that Notre Dame stands tall as the biggest change catalyst of them all. I pushed myself to a higher level of academics *just* to get accepted there.

More than one hundred colleges pursued me because of my speed, strength, and skills as a football player, yet Notre Dame was the only place that bluntly informed me: "You aren't ready academically to come here." That school representative was right. I wasn't good enough. And he did one of the biggest favors anyone has done for me in my life. That wakeup call burned all the way to my inner core. I had to prove that I was good enough.

By doing so, I set the stage for every other change and success in my life. I forced myself to become a better student and a more disciplined person. It took help from a complete campus of supportive people. Teachers, administrators, janitors, coaches, and fellow students all helped push me.

My family and friends all knew about the goal. So did a close acquaintance's father, Larry Hazzard—one of the best ever as a referee in boxing and then commissioner of boxing in New Jersey. God has blessed me with special acquaintances in my life, many of which we are all familiar with.

Notre Dame not only pushed me toward academic excellence and deeper spirituality but also delivered great relationships and a national championship ring. It led me to friends such as Lou Holtz, Leo Hawk, Nicholas Sparks, Gerry Faust, Frank Eck, and Regis Philbin, all of them huge successes in their fields. They have all helped in shaping my life, as have friends like Willis Bright, a retired administrator of the Lilly Foundation in Indianapolis. They have all been confidants and contributors to the Wernle cause.

I participated with the Irish in a unique event a couple of weeks after winning the NCAA Championship, meeting President Reagan and incoming president George Bush Sr. at the White House on the day before the inauguration in 1989. I've played football with dozens of NFL stars, from Tim Brown to Deion Sanders, from Chris Zorich to Frank Stams, and from Ricky Watters to Raghib Ismail.

The Notre Dame campus keeps on giving. And it teaches you—through principles, caring, and spirituality—to give back. I've been blessed to serve as a board member to represent graduates with the Alumni Association and the Monogram Club for former athletes.

Notre Dame's culture brought me undergraduate and graduate degrees and set the stage for my successful pursuit of a law degree. It has led me to my own weekly television show on a Christian station and to a stage where I can reach hundreds of people as a motivational speaker.

The Notre Dame culture helps me every day as a father, a son, a brother, and a friend. It guides me as leader of Wernle.

My life is surrounded by the culture of success that is exuded by Notre Dame. Everything has come full circle.

That campus has brought me wonderful relationships with more people such as Cincinnati lawyer David DeVita, a great friend and mentor who now runs his own firm, and the Maley family—Bob, Charlotte, and John—all of whom have been influential during my time at Wernle.

That campus inspires me with examples of troubled young people who battle every day just to have a normal life. My campuses gave me inspiration and direction when I was struggling. They educated me. They opened my eyes and my opportunities. They introduced me to outstanding people who've helped shape my life.

I've discovered that it takes a "campus of caring" to make lasting changes in your life—positive, ethical, and spiritual people.

There is nothing better than to inspire others to have better lives.

I am here to tell you that you *can* transform yourself.

I am here to help you do that.

ACKNOWLEDGMENTS

THANK YOU TO my high school and college coaches, friends, and family who helped in my transformation of change. None of this would be possible without you.

Thank you to my Notre Dame brothers and sisters who have lifted me up and inspired me on a daily basis.

Thank you to Mike and Julie, who helped make this book a reality.

Thank you to my children, Justis and Darrell Jr., who are the reasons for everything I do.

And thank you, dear reader, for never giving up on your dreams and striving to make them a reality by playing like a champion today.

CHAPTER 1

Flash and the Limelight

I COULD HARDLY imagine what I was seeing—the amazing sights and sounds that surrounded the professional boxing scene. My eyes squinted through the penetrating bright lights as a fog-like mist rose toward the rafters of the huge arena in Atlantic City, New Jersey.

I remember the smell of cigars, the sight of unbelievably beautiful women, and the drenching sense of anticipation centered on the ring. I remember the laughter as men in hats swigged their beers and openly exchanged money as they bet on the outcome of the next match. Everything was electric on this night in a casino-town boxing arena, something few fourteen-year-olds ever get to experience.

Few get to view a boxing match from second-row seats. But I did because my brother Victor was a rising welterweight professional around 1980. He was an amazing athlete who the newspaper columnists said was ticketed for the big time.

He'd take me along sometimes to Atlantic City, where five of his professional bouts were held. We'd stay in a hotel with his trainer, and I'd get to see up close how much people adored Victor. He was so talented, so good-looking, and so easy to be around. Everyone treated him like a movie star.

I knew as I waited that Victor was hidden away in the bowels of the building, getting his hands taped and his face rubbed while listening to pep talks. He never, ever appeared nervous.

Soon he emerged from a slow-moving entourage of people, with the hood of his satiny sweatshirt pulled over his bowed head. His arms rhythmically shadowboxed as he proceeded down the corridor toward the boxing ring. He jumped up and slid in between the ropes as my ears were bombarded by sound.

After a few minutes, the most distinctive words in boxing signal the start: "Get readddddyyyyy to rummmmblllllllllle."

This was a great time for boxing, especially welterweights. Greats such as Sugar Ray Leonard, Roberto Duran, and Thomas Hearns were all in their primes.

Another teenager, heavyweight Mike Tyson, was about ready to hit the scene. Matches were still commonplace on television, and pay-per-view was starting to take off with matches on HBO and Showtime. ESPN was just starting. The scene was electric. People swarmed around up-and-coming boxers.

I was nervous that Victor might lose. I remember cringing and closing my eyes as a flurry of right-handed punches found their mark and sent blood and spit flying. I quickly realized why my mom could never be enticed to watch Victor at a boxing match. The maternal anguish would be too much to bear.

I recall hearing the sharp, distinctive sound of the bell that announced the end of each round and seeing stunning women in bikinis strut placards around to announce round 2. On this night, there was a happy ending. Victor won easily with a knockout, one of many for him.

Imagine being fourteen and taking in this scene several times. It was a preparation for me to be quickly comfortable on another stage in a different dynamic sport.

For example, I was excited, but not awestruck, to run down the tunnel and onto the football field at Notre Dame Stadium just a few years later. And this is the most historic entryway to a field of battle in all of college sports. I was prepared for the sounds, the sights, and the passion. There are no banners; it's pure walls. The famous sign Play Like a Champion, with its blue lettering in gold backdrop, sits above the final turn on the tight stairway that opens onto the stadium tunnel. I was prepared to be a champion, to hear the screams of eighty thousand fans yelling down on the most hallowed grounds of college football.

Big-time boxing matches made me see that big-time dreams were possible. I remember wanting the adulation and the victories, too, that Victor had. But I didn't exactly want to wear the loud and outrageous ensembles of clothing that Victor would strut in around Hillside High School.

"He had such style. No one would say, 'You look like a fool,'" my youngest brother, Chris, said with a laugh while reminiscing recently. "He was unbeaten then. He was going to be the next Sugar Ray or Arguello. Victor made it cool to be outrageous."

I became used to the glamour of high-level athletics by watching and hanging around Victor and my oldest brother, Cedric. It wasn't unusual for me. Cedric was a great football player. They helped mold me to live right and act right. They were instrumental in keeping me from hanging around bad people or making bad decisions. Tragically, their lives spun out of control soon afterward.

Victor helped train Alexis Arguello for his epic battles with Aaron Pryor—both were world champions at various times in their careers—but then dropped off the map as a boxer. "He just couldn't get it back together after losing once or twice," Chris remembers.

I recall that he made such a quick transformation. All of a sudden, he was on the outs. That wasn't even close to his character. I am still amazed. I may never know what the heck happened.

Did he leave the campus, or did the campus leave him? My dad saw problems coming. Some shady people were pushing Victor in his career, and my dad felt that he was being used. That severed their relationship for years.

Chris and I had our parents, although they were divorced by then. But Victor was on his own. Despite his growing successes, I remember him living in a small unappealing apartment. My dad was right: other people made the money off him and then left when the bubble burst.

I could always talk to so many people who wanted to help me. Teammates had such a profound impact.

It brings tears to my eyes when I think of a great thing that happened soon after the boxing night I described above. My father finally went to a fight after months of imploring him. Victor was fighting in a beautiful arena in Jersey City that was just blocks from Dad's business. We convinced him to push aside his father-son problems. I still remember Dad changing out of his mechanic's clothes and into a suit.

We walked in and went to Victor's locker room. We went through, and he was shadowboxing, sweating. "I'm his dad. I want to see my son," he told the people guarding the door.

The scene was really sentimental. My dad walked up and hugged Victor and asked him how he was doing, how he was feeling. That said a lot about what he felt. That wasn't usual. You could tell Victor was happy. We couldn't see their faces, but when they pulled apart, I was certain there were tears in their eyes.

I asked Victor, "Are you ready?"

He answered, "Yeah, I'm ready."

As we took off to find our seats, my dad said, "We'll be in the crowd, cheering you on."

Dad and Victor saw each other just for a moment as Victor entered the ring. They nodded, and I knew they were connected again. That was an amazing moment and an amazing night. Victor won, but the rest of the event remains a blur.

Victor and my older brother, Cedric, shielded Chris and me from the negatives of street life. That was certainly needed because a nasty area of Newark butted up against one side of Hillside. They were my protectors. I climbed on their shoulders.

Cedric is a lot smaller than me, but he was a quick, skilled football player at Hillside High School. I remember going to watch him play and dreamed of starring on that field too. He is outgoing and hardworking—a born businessman like my Dad.

Cedric always loved to get up and go to work with him. My oldest brother inspired me by modeling respect for other people and for running a business. Today, he works in the asbestos-removal business in New Jersey.

As I've mentioned, Victor became a boxer as a teenager and was a welterweight champion in Golden Gloves. He went on to the pro ranks, where he compiled a 13–2 record as a welterweight. Those victories included eleven knockouts.

Victor was relentless in his preparation, something that wore off on me. He'd get up at four each morning to run for several miles in a sweat suit and boots. He'd go next to the basement and hit on a punching bag that was suspended from the ceiling. He'd then go to classes because he was still in high school.

Like Victor, I was gifted physically and was always willing to work out. Seeing his dedication certainly motivated me. I have accomplished some pretty great things in athletics, especially football, but I've never worked as hard as Victor did.

Cedric and Victor always wanted us to let them know if we were being pushed around or if someone offered us drugs or asked us to get involved in something that was against the law. A lot of their efforts, I've been told, happened in the background. They'd tell others not to mess with us.

I always tried to give people the benefit of the doubt and to be nice to everybody, but there was one older boy who constantly pushed me around in our neighborhood. I was shy and didn't enjoy fighting. Finally, I told my older brothers about the bullying. Suffice to say, the bully never bothered me again. I don't know how they made him stop, but I can imagine the scene might have not been real pretty.

One of the ironies of my life is that Victor also carried the nickname Flash. It fit so well for him as a wiry, quick-fisted boxer. He was much smaller than me. The nickname even brought a television station to high school to interview us one time as the "Flash Brothers." It's a nickname that I carry with pride.

Actually, more people called me another name in high school: Abdul. That was a carryover from my flirtations with gang life during late nights in the neighborhood. I assumed the name as a fledgling gang member of thirteen or fourteen with the Arabian Knights in Hillside. Yes, I once was a gang member, a naive and reluctant one. I know now that it was out of youthful ignorance and the need for inclusiveness.

I am very outgoing now, but that wasn't always the case as a youngster. In reality, I was a shy young guy. My smile and good-natured way often hid my insecurities.

Thankfully, I only tested the waters and was never involved in anything that hurt others or myself. In fact, I stayed home the one time our fledgling young gang was supposed to fight with another, with fists and weapons, on a street in Newark.

As I previously mentioned, one of the foremost truisms I've learned in life—from the streets of New Jersey to Notre Dame to now—is that major changes often are the result of a severe degree of discomfort. I was fearful of many things. In fact, it's one of the great ironies of my life that I didn't lust for collisions even though my college football career as an outside linebacker often depended on them.

I made interceptions and fumble recoveries and dozens of tackles at Notre Dame, but my greatest individual memories are of making sacks of the quarterback. I still dream of rushing in and making a play that brings a roar inside Notre Dame Stadium. I never gained pleasure from inflicting pain. It was a game. If you knock someone down, it's just as important to reach out a hand to help him up. Sometimes it's good to have a little fear.

Being in a gang went against everything my mother and father preached and what I instinctively believed in. There really was no room in my life for the anger, the drug use, and the senseless violence.

Many of my close childhood friends were inclined toward the gang world, though. And all young people want inclusion. Sad to say, many are in jail, addicted to drugs. Many are dead.

I often wonder what happened to all my junior high friends, and I am so thankful that I was presented with other opportunities. I had seen chains and knives and the occasional gun in the hands of young people during our gang get-togethers. Chris said, "There were a lot of influences and directions to not do the right thing. There were a lot of temptations." Looking back, I can see why it's so easy to be in a gang, to be a follower rather than a leader. But it's such a trap.

One critical point of my story is that you can be a leader rather than a follower—that you can follow through with the major changes that are needed to achieve a more fulfilling and successful life. You can follow your dreams no matter your position in life.

A healthy dose of fear helped me to permanently pull away from the streets and gangs. So did the realization early in high school that

I was a gifted athlete. God granted me size, quickness, and strength. He granted me a quick mind to grasp the teaching moments from my coaches. I played football, basketball, and ran track, and I was so busy that I didn't have time for anything that could get me in trouble. That helped end the gang affiliation, but it didn't stop people from calling me Abdul.

I think many of the friends who turned to the gangs wouldn't bother me because they wanted to bask in the glow of sports successes too. They understood that was my role. They enjoyed cheering on Hillside High School's teams and took pride in the school's victories.

People today still call me Abdul or Ab when I am back home. Nicknames are an important part of culture. I am Flash to those who followed me at Notre Dame. I am Mr. Gordon to the students at Wernle Youth & Family Treatment Center. These humorous and prescient comments were made in my senior yearbook by Coach Larry Coppola. They illustrate the nickname situation perfectly:

> Darrell, Flash, Ab or whatever your name is: It was a real experience getting to know you for 4 years. You performed exceptionally well on the field when you remembered your jersey, helmet & cleats. Thanks to you I got to meet Joe Paterno & Gerry Faust. It was a tough decision but I think you made a good one. IRISH WILL BE # 1. You better keep in touch and remember your old coach. I will never forget you no matter how hard I try. Keep eating & lifting. (Coach Larry Coppola)

Coach Coppola was a great help in my life. He was always watching out for my health and welfare.

Regrettably, I don't think my brother Victor received caring guidance from those around him. He was used in his boxing career. I can't help but wonder if many of Victor's current challenges aren't related to the cumulative effect of getting punched in the head so many times.

We participated in sports in a different era. If an athlete today shows even a hint of a concussion, he or she is held out of action. You see it all the time now on televised football games.

That was seldom the case in my playing days of the 1980s. We called it getting our bell rung, and we went back into action as soon as the cobwebs cleared, sometimes after being jerked back to consciousness by smelling salts.

Think of how many times boxers get hit in the head. I think Victor is lucky to be alive. It hurts that he isn't with me more now and that we aren't close.

His leadership was so essential to my life. It motivated me to see him succeed. He fought at least one hundred times in his amateur and professional careers. He even had a bout against a fellow student from Hillside High School, in the school gym. I was so proud when he easily won. The praise showered down on me and on the Gordon family, as well as Victor. I wanted to be like him—to succeed on a big stage.

Thankfully, I got the chance to do so.

CHAPTER 2

Parents Model Change

EVEN THOUGH I have never lived there, South Carolina serves as the seed for any successes, any bright lights, that I have encountered in my life. The lush farm fields and family ties of South Carolina represent a heritage of hard work, hope, and change that were always a part of my identity.

My father, Roosevelt, would always talk about moving up to New Jersey as a teenager. My mother, Helen, came north, too, in the great migration toward better job opportunities. My parents didn't know each other before they came, but they shared the hardworking ethics and dreams that served as the backbone of our country and our family.

It wasn't easy to leave their families and the only homes they had known. My dad still travels back there frequently. But they both knew very well that there were few opportunities to advance for black teenagers in the South of the 1950s.

My father's ambitions were strong as he sweated through his daily chores as a child on the farm. He ran tractors and cultivators by the time he was twelve years old. The premature death of his father had dictated that my dad quit school after the eighth grade. The simple fact then was that it was far more productive for him to work full-time on the farm than continue toward a high school degree.

His schooling stopped, but he never stopped learning. He's always had an intuitive and inquisitive nature. He soaked up knowledge from watching people as well as reading books. He studied how engines worked and was fascinated by them. He also studied people and the latest trends.

All these factors ignited a dream to run his own service station far away from where he grew up. "I wanted a better life, and I felt like I could get it," he said from his home near Newark.

He obviously carried many natural attributes besides working hard. He was smart. He was honest. He was confident. And he was fearless about making major changes.

He made a gigantic one at age seventeen that forever transformed his life and affected the lives of my four brothers, my two sisters, and me. He headed to an area of New Jersey that sits across the Hudson River, in the shadows of the Manhattan skyline. Eventually, he and four siblings relocated there: sisters Sue, Alice, and Polly, and a brother, Herbert.

My dad first landed work in New Jersey in a laundromat and was paid a dollar an hour to remove the collar stains out of clients' business shirts. That doesn't sound like much now, but he explained, "A dollar meant something then."

A gallon of gas or milk cost about twenty cents in the mid-1950s, and apartment rent was about thirty-five dollars a month. A friend introduced him to a loving, driven, and spirit-filled woman named Helen Daisey. They soon had a lot more in common than a South Carolina heritage. They would marry and build a family together—first a daughter, Charnette, and then four sons, Cedric, Victor, me, and Chris. My father also has a daughter, Doris, and a son, Philip Jackson, from other relationships.

Helen worked in a textile factory. The salary there wasn't large, but it was better than what she could have earned in South Carolina. East New Jersey offered an abundance of churches, apartments, and new acquaintances. There were endless stores, theaters, and restaurants.

But there were also big-city problems, such as drug abuse and violence. Dad soon found a better job as a mechanic at the post office in Jersey City. He enjoyed working there and could probably have stayed for decades. But the thirst to drink the American Dream couldn't be quenched there.

He opened a service station in West New York, New Jersey, a spot where almost every customer was white. That didn't matter to him or to the large majority of his satisfied customers. What mattered was service, dignity, and respect.

Dad knew the venom of racism very well during the 1960s—an explosive period of race relations in the United States. He chose, instead, to focus on virtues such as honesty and character. He modeled that to each of his children, all of whom worked with him when they got old enough. "I get the drive from him," said Chris, my younger brother. "He didn't go to high school, yet he provided for his children with a keen knowledge and instincts about business and life."

Dad taught his children that being black certainly would affect their futures, but their actions and good deeds ultimately would determine their fates. He would teach and lead, then get out of the way. He instinctively knew that racial bigotry would be quieted with righteous deeds and sacrifice, not with rage, riots, and violence. "You have good and bad in all races," he would tell me often.

He surprisingly found that it was his customers who dressed down fellow white people when they crossed the boundaries of racial decency and failed to show the respect due any hardworking American man. "I was really impressed by his moderate way, his inclusive way of seeing the black experience," Chris remembers.

Dad befriended common folks, community leaders, and company presidents alike. He'd invite some of them along to special family occasions, such as sporting events and graduations. Family and friends marvel that he was always able to get banks to help finance his projects. You don't make that happen without having deep support systems.

He just wanted to be treated like any other businessman and had obviously earned the trust and respect of bank officers. After about a decade, Dad bought a building that stretched almost a city block. He started running a shop that serviced trucks. It was a place where all his kids worked on weekends and during summer vacations.

His piece of urban land included a huge area that he rented out for parking tractor-trailer trucks, which aren't easy to park in the congested streets of urban New Jersey and New York. He rented a second floor to an accounting firm. Ironically, the site was purchased from him in the last decade and turned into a modern and new public school campus.

In the early 1970s, we moved to Hillside, a town of 21,000 about ten miles west of Jersey City that sits in the shadows of Newark Airport. Hillside was much roomier, airier, and safer than where we were living in a big apartment home in an increasingly crime-ridden area of Jersey City. Hillside was kind of an oasis tucked between rougher areas of Newark and its suburbs. "There was a better house, a better class of people, and better education for our children in Hillside," Dad said.

Hillside and surrounding suburban towns offered diversity, where races existed more in harmony than in separate ways. It was the home headquarters of Bristol Myers-Squibb and Lionel Trains. It was the hometown of Yankees' great Phil Rizzuto, writer Philip Roth, comedian-actor Jerry Lewis, and real estate magnate Zygi Wilf, who owns the Minnesota Vikings. My mom strongly supported the move because it offered better opportunities for the main focus of her life—her five children. Hillside offered a community swimming pool, open fields for Pop Warner football programs, a big municipal library, and close proximity to highways and commuter railways.

My parents modeled leadership. Hard work and honesty were expectations. So were character and a higher mission in life. Without the determination and the life-changing moments embraced by them, I am certain I would never have discovered the campuses that have carried me to so many positive places.

My parents also modeled parenting and the community that is the root of all campuses.

I smile every day with memories of my mom, who embraced me and embarrassed me so many times with her love. She would come flying out the door with her housecoat billowing and her head covered with a hairnet. "Darrrelllll, it's time for dinnnnner!" she'd yell. She usually didn't have to yell more than once for me to come home.

Everyone on the streets knew my mom was looking for me—neighbors, friends, everyone. It simply was time for me to go. It would be disrespectful not to head home. It was a natural process that repeated itself each time a beckoning call bellowed out from the mouths of moms and dads who cared.

It was like that for decades, but I'm not sure it's happening anymore. I'm not sure families are surrounding their children like that. It's a major reason that I have dedicated myself to providing a safe haven for kids at Wernle Youth & Family Treatment Center. We need campuses of caring, whether it's a neighborhood home or a residential home, for troubled children. Kids need a place to come home to.

Within moments after my mom's "Darrrelllll, it's time for dinnnnner" proclamation, word would start spreading down the street and eventually reach up to one of the parks, where I could often be found playing basketball. Some parks were more than a mile away. Neighbors would tell their kids to run up and tell me to head home, or they'd start a telephone tree to get the message out.

There were no cell phones or iPads then. Word of mouth was the network, and it worked very well indeed. People talked to one another face-to-face. Our neighborhood then was no different than many across the nation. People watched out for one another. My neighbors didn't laugh at my mom. In fact, many of the neighborhood moms slipped into their housecoats when they got home from exhausting days working in factories just like she did.

My mom often worked two jobs while we were growing up. Times were tight.

When I got the word, either by hearing my mom's distinctive yells or from a buddy passing up the message, I'd immediately head home.

One reason was the fear of my mom's wrath (and the switch in her hand). Another was my respect for her. And the other was because I have always had a big appetite. She sometimes fed all my brothers and sisters and our friends too. And all of us could clean a plate very quickly. Our house always smelled good in the evening. We'd seldom eat out. It was too expensive, and the family table was so important.

There'd be huge pots steaming with spaghetti noodles and the sweet smells of sausage and sauces. We'd go through gallons of milk and juices each day. The smells of breads and desserts mingled with the entrées. I can still close my eyes and recall the heavenly aroma.

Charnette often cooked, too, especially if my mom was late. She played a strong big-sister role in pushing me toward big successes in my life. She really was the model glue for our family. She was so fun and energetic. She loved life and loved people.

As the oldest child and only girl in our nuclear family, Charnette was often called upon to watch Chris and me when we were young. She truly did everything for us. She was there to keep us grounded, just like a mom. Charnette was always there to cook meals, dispense advice, encourage us to be good students, and escort us to our practices and ballgames.

There was always a lot of attention paid to us when Chris and I were around her. Everybody loved my sister. She was very attractive, nice, and kind. She was very strong academically. The teachers really liked her. Charnette's popularity was evident by the fact she was voted Homecoming Queen at Hillside High during her senior year.

My stepsister, Doris, hung around our house a lot and stood as another great example of how to live right. She and Charnette were best friends. Charnette played a strong role in encouraging Chris and me to go on to college. It would bring us a better life, she'd say. And she was right. She was an inspiration. She set many of the trails for us to follow.

She was actually the first person in our family to attend college. She had learned about bookkeeping by working for my dad. We all worked for him in some way or another. She went to work for a bank, which helped her take some classes at Kean College. I remember that was a huge source of pride for my parents, my siblings, and me.

She always encouraged me to think bigger and was a huge supporter for me in going to Notre Dame. Charnette visited Africa several times with a man she was dating, so she wasn't fearful of going out into the world.

One of the proudest moments of my life came when Charnette and many other family members came out to watch Notre Dame play a game at the Meadowlands in my freshman year. Coach Gerry Faust allowed me to travel with the team, even though I was redshirting that year because of an injury. Faust was good about that kind of thing.

Making successful moves and life changes became a driving stimuli for Chris and me. As the youngsters in the family, we had the luxury of watching and learning from the successes and mistakes of our parents and older siblings.

Mom was the spiritual rock of our home—the mother bear in a housecoat whose role was to protect, nurture, and discipline. My dad, Roosevelt Gordon, epitomized the honest, hardworking, businessman who provided for his family.

My parents drifted apart while I was young and eventually divorced, yet they never strayed from modeling what was right in life. A divorce can really hurt children, but my parents worked hard not to allow that to happen. They worked together on parenting, despite their differences. Chris and I had the advantage of being young when my parents split.

It certainly hit my older brothers harder. There was a four-year separation between Victor and me, while I am almost seven years older than Chris.

The age separations proved to be a huge benefit for both of us. It was natural that Chris identified with me more than Cedric and Victor. They were ten and eleven years older than him. I ended my career at

Hillside and headed to Notre Dame just as he was ending his time in junior high school.

"I did a lot of watching of all of my brothers and sisters. One consistent brother was you," Chris said recently. "You had a schedule. Work out, study, and go to practice. You definitely were one of my biggest mentors at a young age. I was always in awe of how you led your life in relation to my other brothers. You had aspirations so much bigger than the town we grew up in. That influenced me."

We were drawn closer, I'm sure, because of my parents' split. Both of us believe strongly that we were fortunate that our father was still in our lives.

Our mom came to play a stronger day-to-day role. "I like to think of her as a martyr," Chris said. "She gave up her life for her children. She just wanted us to grow up, be healthy and happy, and make grandchildren. Her legacy was about her children." Mom was a consensus builder. Chris said, "She taught me about love, about having a big heart. She brought people together. She was so diplomatic. I got that from my mom."

Chris and I are close yet very different in our personalities. I am outgoing. "You were always that way," Chris said. "You were always very happy to meet people, to find out where they are from, what their plans were. People love you. You don't have to fake it to be a nice guy."

The athletic genes, the family modeling, and my own determination carried me to a full-ride scholarship at Notre Dame. Chris was a great player, too, but earned his way to Brown University on academics alone. That Ivy League school gained a huge plus when he went there. Chris played as a star linebacker and captain on the football team.

Both of us revel in reaching broad audiences, albeit in entirely different ways. I am doing so as a motivational speaker and advocate for young people. He is doing so by helping set up major exhibitions at museums across the United States. He also is a writer and producer of cable television programs in Hollywood. Chris is content to do his work in branding, marketing, and product development in the background.

Our different styles make for great long conversations and, yes, sometimes arguments. But with love and respect, we both keep learning from each other. We are lucky to have each other and a family whose members value change as a tool for reaching a better life.

Chris's graduation day was one I will never forget because our mom was there. She couldn't attend my graduations at Notre Dame due to financial reasons. In fact, due to financial constraints, she never saw me play a football game live for the Irish. She was content, instead, to stay home and watch the games on television. Looking back, that is a real hole in my life—a major regret. The long tunnel leading to the football field at Notre Dame is so special. It's filled with people on game days as the players worked their way down. All the parents are there. That was the fruits of their labor. Dad came several times a year.

I made it a point to take Mom to Chris's graduation at Brown. I wanted her to see what it was like to be on a campus. Singer Diana Ross's daughter was graduating at the same time. That made it even more special. Thankfully, Mom got the opportunity then to see what the campus experience was all about—that it was a reflection of our upbringing. She was so thrilled for us, and we were so thrilled to see her smile and share in such a momentous achievement.

I can think about that at any time and just hear her saying, "Darrelllll and Chrrrrrissssss, you did our family right."

Mom focused a lot of special attention on me for many years. Her spirituality enveloped me like a warm blanket on a cold winter night. She made sure that I had a spiritual connection from the start. My earliest memories revolve around church as much as my home life.

Mom showed me the way. She never let me down even though I let her down many times. I never used drugs, but I did dabble in gang life. She insisted on living right and doing lots of praying every day. That model always has served as a big comfort for me.

If I had a major challenge, a big class test, or the SAT while in high school, I knew I could ask my mom, "Could you pray for me?" We had what you'd call blessing oil. She used to put that on my forehead so I could bring Christ with me. I'd ask for her to apply it to me. When your teenager comes and asks you to do that, she had to know that the special spiritual training she had given me had paid off. That spirituality meant attending services—with hearty preaching and emotional music for hours on end—on Sundays and Wednesday nights at the Cotton Temple Church of God in Jersey City, New Jersey.

That Pentecostal church rocked with emotion and the righteous Word of God. Mom and I always went to the earliest services. It became quite an undertaking, though, after we moved from Jersey City to Hillside. Our new home was an hour away on the congested roads around Newark that lead into New York City.

Cotton Temple had been Mom's church since before I was born. Nothing would keep us from going there. She'd always drive, often twice on Sundays. She wanted someone with her, and I was always ready to go. I never had a chance to ask her why I was the one who usually accompanied her. But I can guess that my two older brothers were more challenging, and Charnette often stayed home to care for Chris, who was born shortly after we moved to Hillside.

Maybe I was just more receptive to my mom's exhortations because of God's will. There certainly were a few times when I didn't like going to church so much. No young child likes to sit for hours on hard pews while wearing hot, itchy dress-up clothes.

I can't tell you how many times I remember my mom saying, "Stop acting out," during the three hours of Sunday school and services. Admittedly, I would sometimes detour from attending Sunday school with my friends and cousins. We'd sneak down the street to buy candy at the corner store.

My mom had a secret weapon to keep me in tow, though, as she modeled God's Word. "After church, we'll go to McDonald's," she'd say with a wink. I always straightened up because I loved spending that special time with her. She always followed through on her promise.

I realize more as each year goes by how committed my mom was to stay with her church. The strength of other Cotton Temple members was amazing too. The big stone building was in the middle of an area that grew increasingly drug and crime ridden from the 1960s up to the early 1990s. That grim issue is what helped drive my parents to move to Hillside in the first place. Members at Cotton Temple believed in the power of salvation in the midst of savagery. So they stayed where they could make a difference.

The model of Cotton Temple's goodness and righteousness stays with me today. Now it's my son, Darrell Jr., who is nine years old and squirming at church on Sunday mornings. But it's part of our life, as is constant praying.

My family attends the first church service at 9:00 AM each Sunday because we want to have a full day in front of us to push the positive message into other areas of our lives. The spiritual time serves as a catalyst for the day and the week ahead.

I am becoming more and more spiritual over time. So much of that is a reflection of my mother. We start a lot of meetings off in prayer at Wernle. It might go something like this: "Can we just have a prayer for us that Wernle does well, that I can continue to lead in a positive fashion?"

I want faith to be present, just like my mother's everlasting goodness and faith are with me every day. She was such a caring, calming influence, even as she was going through the trauma of the breakup with my father.

We could easily tell that their relationship was dysfunctional. That's rough on kids of young ages. You witness the fights and the yelling and you notice—and are fearful—when one parent doesn't come home at night. If Dad promised a customer that a car would be ready the next morning, he'd work all night to make that happen.

My parents still talked about things and argued sometimes after their split, but overall, Mom was so into Christ that she focused on that relationship. Mom ruled the roost at home and was definitely the authoritative person. Deadlines weren't to be missed, nor were chores or church services. She was always about being prepared, looking good, and being appropriate.

Her overprotection in front of our friends and neighbors was a bit embarrassing at times, but as a parent now, I see how much she cared for us and tried to point us down the right paths. She would not let us compromise our values. That meant she wanted to know the friends that her children were hanging around with. She had a great nose for knowing the kids who could be bad news. Her instincts helped her drive away some of those who were pushing me toward being a gang member.

So did my father, who insisted we work with him on the weekends whenever we could. He taught me about being customer-friendly and doing the job right. I learned to smile and be polite. I changed tires, pumped gas, and washed windows—anything that was needed. I was doing billing at his shop at the age of fourteen. That was work, but it was far easier than what my father was doing at the same age on the family farm in South Carolina.

I remember deciding that I wanted to do something big in life—to lead other people—while working at my dad's shop. I first dreamed of becoming a CEO because of my dad. He pushed his children to be the best and treated us all equally.

My dad didn't accept excuses. You were given a job, and you did it. If something didn't work, you fix it. You learned from your failures.

Mom would fret about us doing things such as burning our hands on a hot stove. My father, on the other hand, was more the realist. He believed in letting us learn from our mistakes. His philosophy is that you can't be protective of everything. If a child touches a hot burner once, it would never happen again. He or she would learn or keep getting burned.

Their differences were stark in my middle school years, the most at-risk time of my life. I was extremely shy and reserved through childhood. I was always pleasant around people, always had a ready smile, but some of that hid the fact that I was afraid that I wouldn't succeed.

Sports helped bring me out of my shell. I was quick, athletic, and savvy on the football field. As I became more confident, I became more sociable around other people.

It made me feel so good when folks started calling me Flash because I did so well in Pop Warner football. But a fear of failure—and the pain of being tackled—pushed me to run faster as much as my talent did. I had a good reason to fear pain: my football career nearly ended on a Pop Warner field when I was about thirteen years old.

I had just scored a touchdown when an opponent surprisingly tripped me from behind. I fell awkwardly, and when I looked down, my arm wasn't where it should be. I was shocked. I had a fractured elbow. Soon, a horrible pain kicked in. My mom decided while I was being treated at the hospital that I was finished forever with football.

She was my biggest fan. She'd sit in the bleachers even at practices when she didn't have to work. I was so proud to know she was there. But part of the reason was her overprotective nature. It hurt her too much when I got hurt badly. So she made up her mind that I must stop playing football as the full-length cast was being placed on my arm.

I begged to let me play for many months after that, but she didn't even want me to participate in pickup games with friends from the neighborhood. I think she would have been fine if I stayed home and never played another sport. I sometimes wonder what I'd be doing now if that injury had indeed ended my sports career. Would I have found other campuses of learning, other pathways to success?

Who knows? But that football injury was no different than any major event that happens and forces you to make a change. Broken arms, concussions, knee injuries, and a lot worse happen every week to thousands of athletes.

Some never get the chance to play again. Thank God I won the battle to play again with pivotal help from my dad.

I remember him telling my mom, "Let him go out and play. Getting hurt is part of the game. He'll be stronger for it."

My father was right. Thankfully, my mother finally relented. Learning to overcome obstacles is a major factor in having successes in life. People can't avoid risks. They should always push toward their dreams and cultivate their strengths.

Chris said he watched what happened with me and wanted to emulate my experiences. Fortunately, we both were able to keep playing football and stay away from the gang life that has such a negative stranglehold on major cities across the United States.

It's amazing to think of all the factors—all the campuses, coaches, teachers, and family members—that contributed to my wonderful life.

None would have been possible without the life-altering decision to move to New Jersey and perseverance by my parents more than a decade before I was born in 1966.

My achievements can all be traced back to them.

CHAPTER 3

Seeds of Change in High School

IT WAS HEADY times, light-shining fun times, as a junior at Hillside High School. I would walk the halls with a confident step. Everybody knew me. Everybody knew I was the brother of Victor, a nationally known boxer.

But I was a star in my own right on the football field and in the basketball gym. Our football team was awesome. We won most of our games with ease. Just one close loss kept us from a shot at a state championship.

I was strong and fast at six feet three and 190 pounds, making sack after sack on defense and running for lots of touchdowns on offense. I could bench press more than twice my body weight. Working out in the weight room was simple to me. I could always force myself to get up early to run and lift weights. I had been watching Victor do it for years. I wanted to be in the glittering lights like him.

Truth to tell, my favorite sport was basketball. Hillside was very good at that, too, with waves of gifted athletes. Screaming fans would fill our little old gym as we won game after game.

I could imagine more of the same at college at either sport. I could imagine myself starring in college and then making big money as a pro athlete. The problem was, I didn't have the proper academic focus as a junior. I wasn't preparing for my future life as a student, a national champion, and eventually a CEO. I simply didn't know how.

One single negative event helped give me that focus and changed my life for the rest of my life. Notre Dame didn't want me when they first checked into my background. The simple reason was that I didn't fit their academic model. I hadn't proven that I had what it would take to succeed there. I was good enough with my football skills. That gift alone could have landed me at any of one hundred or more universities.

But Notre Dame expects to graduate every player it recruits, and it succeeds 98 percent of the time. Academics are rigorous there. Being snubbed at first and being told that I wasn't good enough academically yet became the biggest single factor in propelling me on the positive path that has since defined my life. I realized I had to make a major change just to get Notre Dame to consider me.

There's a lot more to that crucial story, but first let me chat a bit about that era to set the stage better. It was a different world when I was in high school in the early 1980s—one that my young children, ages thirteen and nine, couldn't even fathom today. The same goes for any high school student or traditional college student.

We didn't have cell phones, emails, or iPads. We didn't have social networking sites such as YouTube and Facebook. There was no Skype or LinkedIn. Heck, there was no internet that offered unlimited bits of information and instant gratification. Today's communications conveniences were as much science fiction to us as the *Star Wars* movies that enthralled me as a child. We knew the cartoonish Tweety bird, not the 140-character tweets on Twitter.

In fact, Bill Gates was just getting started on Microsoft in the fall of 1982 when I started my junior year of high school. ESPN, CNN, MTV, and the Weather Channel were still in their infancies. I don't remember anyone in my neighborhood having cable television. That simply was a luxury we couldn't afford.

Even without those distractions, I still had trouble concentrating. My body was filled with nonstop energy. My son is the same way: a great motor and an active mind. There's a big difference between having a sharp mind and putting it to best use. The same goes for having an athletic body and having energy to spare. You have to find the proper ways to channel them.

There was another major difference in the high school environment of the 1980s: no huge societal push toward doing homework and testing benchmarks. That left a lot of free time when I wasn't taking part in sports after school. Some of that were taken up with working for my dad at his auto shop. Some were taken up following Victor as he pursued a career in boxing.

Most of my time outside of school and family functions was taken up with athletics at school or on the playgrounds near my home. I played organized football in the fall and basketball in the winter. Like many athletes then, I participated in sports around the year. One reason was that the football and basketball coaches also coached other sports. There wasn't the year-round focus on a single sport. I participated in track during the spring because I was needed to fill out the squad and was a strong athlete, not because I liked throwing the shot put or discus. I enjoyed being around my friends.

Looking back, I see that our coaches had other motives. They wanted to keep us busy and off the streets as we got older. There were bad influences out there, and it was too easy to give in to them.

Besides those athletic activities, though, we played outside after school. That had happened since childhood. We played pickup basketball and tossed footballs and baseballs by the hour. It was nothing for me to walk a mile to join a basketball game at a park or community gymnasium.

Notre Dame's initial snub in the fall of 1982 forced me to realize the importance of getting top-notch grades. I forced myself to step up. It took lots of help along the way from teachers, coaches, and mentors. Now I realize that I was focused on too many fun things as a youngster and had too many distractions. That's a common theme, of course, with millions of young students of any background. I see it every day with the residents at Wernle Youth & Family Treatment Center. The distractions are only getting worse with the latest new gadgets.

I was honored to be designated a captain in football, basketball, and track. That meant that coaches considered me a leader. But my leadership qualities and athletic skills alone weren't going to get me within sniffing distance of playing football and attending classes on the beautiful Notre Dame campus in South Bend, Indiana.

The majority of students at Notre Dame are the cream of the academic crop. The university cares so much about its athletic recruits that it studies their academic backgrounds as well as their on-field exploits before offering scholarships. That's why a Notre Dame representative was sent to sift through my academic records at Hillside.

I wasn't an honor roll student, but I had never flunked a class. I always had a quick mind about grasping most subjects in school. But, again, I didn't have the focus I needed. The representative informed administrators and coaches that I hadn't displayed the academic prowess that I'd need to succeed at Notre Dame. It was that simple. He didn't even take the time to talk to me. That shocked me to the core of my being.

As I've mentioned before, one of my favorite sayings is that major changes often happen only after undergoing a significant degree of discomfort. I have felt the severe discomfort many times, none more than at this critical point in my life. Notre Dame lit a fire in me before I ever really knew what that university stood for or even where it was located. Before the representative's visit, I thought I was the king of Hillside—that athletics would take me to great heights of fame and money.

That junior year was also profound in another way: I sustained a slow-healing ankle injury in my senior year, which seriously impacted my play. My statistics were nothing compared to my junior season. That same ankle caused me to miss playing in my first year at Notre Dame. If that hadn't happened, though, I wouldn't have gotten a fifth season and would have missed out on playing in the championship season.

Fortune can play critical roles in your life.

I needed a perfect storm of positive things to happen in that fall of 1982 for me to even get the chance to attend Notre Dame. If I had waited to show my skills athletically and academically, other opportunities could have passed me by. I learned at that juncture of my life that you have to make serious changes at times in your life to move ahead. You must sacrifice what you are for what you want to become.

You need discipline and to work hard to achieve in the variety of life arenas that define success. You have to honor the gifts you have, find those who can help you achieve, and make your own breaks to make good things happen. Just as you can't succeed by yourself, your athletic talents alone won't take you to the top.

Whenever I visit young people about athletic dreams, I always ask them if they know the odds for a high school football player to ever play in the NFL. Boys and girls raised their hands and shouted out their thoughts recently when I visited Calvin Coolidge Elementary in Hillside. Most guessed it's 1 in 100 or 1 in 500. You could hear an audible gasp when I said it's more like 1 in 10,000. Even if they make it to the NFL, I told them, the average career lasts only a little more than three years (according to statistics from the NFL Players Association).

It was fun to visit the kids and rekindle ties with Bob Enda, who coached me in high school and was a teacher at Coolidge. He has become a dear friend and mentor. Children need to hear from people who have succeeded and to hear that dreams of making it big in sports aren't realistic, Enda told me during the visit. I was certain that I could play in the NFL, and top coaches told me I certainly had the skills. But I never got the chance because of an injury which I'll divulge more about later.

The eye-opening visit by the Notre Dame representative paid one of the greatest dividends in my life just six years later when we won the title at Notre Dame. I couldn't have made it without the impetus of being told I wasn't good enough academically. It wasn't easy to stay home to study on many weekends and on late nights after practices in high school. It meant giving up a lot of fun times. But I was so afraid that I had blown any chance of going to Notre Dame.

However, I succeeded in pulling my grades higher, and Coach Gerry Faust finally called to personally offer me a scholarship. It's funny, when you look back on critical points in your life, how changes can happen quickly or slowly. They can pile up and build you up or push you down.

Picture yourself walking upstairs in a very tall building. You reach one landing and then head up another. You can't climb all the stairs at the same time. Yet each step leads to another. Sometimes, you have to stop on one landing for a while or even go back down before climbing again. It's the same in everyday life with the challenges you face. Nothing I have now would have been possible without accepting more challenges and making more changes all along the way.

The seeds of my motivational speaking techniques were sown in that junior year.

I had many catalysts for change in high school. Teachers, coaches, and administrators encouraged me daily as I pushed toward my goal of being accepted by Notre Dame. They knew about it because I told them. It helped immeasurably to have a strong support system—family, friends, teachers, coaches, mentors, and more. It's impossible to name everyone who helped me. But, stand assured, it took the whole high school campus, a focused educational atmosphere, to lead me to Notre Dame and beyond.

I was encouraged and pushed to succeed by even the kitchen workers and custodians once it became known that I had an opportunity to go to Notre Dame. People would yell out there cars or from the stands in support for me making it. In a way, the whole town of Hillside picked me up, pushed me to succeed, and gave me unbelievable support. The community wanted me to make it.

It helped, too, to have some great classmates who were models of leadership.

Longtime friend and teammate Dwayne Rush served as a great model for me—a true leader in academics and sports, actually everything he did. We competed all the time from grammar school up to high school. He was a natural and an awesome quarterback in football and point guard in basketball. He also was an A student. He went on to play football at Florida A&M, earned an MBA at Harvard, and worked on Wall Street. We'd hang out together all the time and eat at each other's houses. His mom, like mine, was an awesome cook and a model of caring. I've been fortunate to play with many great people, but none better than him.

I was fortunate to realize at a young age that I didn't have all the answers. I had to lean on some people to find successes. I didn't know where I was going, but I knew I wanted to go somewhere good. I wanted to be good and accomplish good things.

I gravitated to leaders to find the way to success. Following are many folks who served as my closest confidants:

- *Steve Kleiman, history teacher.* He was a great friend to my family and me. He first counseled my brother, Victor, who, as you know, was a champion boxer and a senior when I was a freshman in high school. He started following us and our sports exploits while at the same time serving as a strong teacher.
- *Alonzo Taylor (Mr. Z), physics teacher.* I remember doing experiments, blowing stuff up in his classes. It was rare to get kudos from a teacher then, but he was committed to me. I still remember him saying the last time we saw each other, "Good luck in all you do. I know that you'll do well."
- *Althea Williams, senior class adviser.* I was fortunate to have her in middle school and then in high school too. Truth to tell,

I had a little crush on her when I first met her in the eighth grade at George Washington School. She was so supportive in helping me through the selection process for classes. That was so essential because any misstep could have hurt my chances of qualifying for an NCAA Division I football program. Althea obviously knew about grooming young scholar-athletes. Her son, Jay, was a basketball star at Duke and went on to play in the NBA.

- *Joe Silver, athletic director and basketball coach.* He stressed so many things to his players besides constant defensive pressure. He'd buy the players doughnuts for Saturday practices. That was a huge treat for a lot of us. It made us bond and feel more special. I remembered he'd always hand out vitamin C tablets and make us wear hats when we left the gym on cold nights. He was trying to protect us. You can't play well if you are sick.
- My coaches did a lot to keep players busy and out of trouble. For example, Coach Silver would have one of his friends drive five or six of us around town in his station wagon after games and on weekends. That served many purposes. It bonded the players. It also let the coaches know where we were and controlled the time we got home. It protected us.
- *Alfred Lordi, assistant principal, and William Todt, vice principal.* Those two were mainstays in my high school growth. Lordi was one of the closest to my family. They must have seen something in me. I really came to trust both of them for their advice and leadership. They were older, wiser, and very firm in their discipline. They both had an affinity for me, a commitment to me.

Their commitment to me included suspending me for several days in my senior year. Say what? It bears explaining. I punched a guy during study hall. I have never been oppositional, but these guys were playing around, throwing things, as I was trying to study. One guy threw a wad of paper that accidentally hit me, and I simply snapped because this group had been abusing others in the class. I wanted no part of that, but I thought it had to be stopped.

My intentions were pure. I wanted them to know that I was off-limits and that I shouldn't be messed with. But my reaction certainly crossed the line. I quickly learned how fragile something like that can turn out. I could have really hurt the kid. It could have been seen as battery. I could have ended up in jail with a record. It's not a football game or practice, where you hit people as a matter of course and can even get into scraps once in a while. You just can't retaliate in that way in school or anywhere. It's something I never did again.

I avoid confrontations. Those are battles that I can never win. Luckily, I learned my lesson, and my punishment was suspension, not getting expelled or going to court. To this day, I wonder what happened to those rowdy kids from study hall. I pray they are having wonderful lives.

It bothers me that so many young people don't respect one another enough to be polite. They don't respect the law. They don't respect one another. I think people who don't respect and fear laws compromise their morals. People who don't respect the legal system should scare you. A love for the American legal system is what attracted me to law school, and it certainly came in valuable in landing my job as leader at Wernle Youth & Family Treatment Center in 2001.

Many of the residents at Wernle are one or two steps away from incarceration. It's our mission to help change them, to offer them hope and tools for a better future. A strong part of that mission is education. All our students are attending high school or middle school or working toward their GEDs. We show that we care, like all those educators who helped guide me as an impressionable young man showed me. Our residents are at critical turning points in their lives. The courses of their futures will be determined in large part by the positives we can impart upon them. Their circumstances are different, but the point is the same. We all need to be loved and pushed to have better lives—to keep climbing the stairs to a more fruitful and fulfilling life.

CHAPTER 4

The Recruiting Story

BEING RECRUITED BY Notre Dame was like having that person you've long admired say yes to your invitation to the prom. It's the answer to dreams and prayers. Everything was honest and aboveboard with Notre Dame in the whole process. The university offered so much—the bright lights and the title opportunities that I desired as a football player. The bright future and educational opportunities that I needed to move forward after my playing career. The caring, cajoling, and Christian-based leadership of coaches and instructors. The family atmosphere and spiritual grounding that my soul (and my parents) so desired.

The campus environment appealed above other colleges with an immediate feeling of family and fatherly direction. God is present everywhere on campus. In fact, there are worship centers in every building.

I'd be lying, though, if I didn't say I was tempted about playing elsewhere.

In fact, I was heavily recruited by Coach Joe Paterno and his staff to play at Penn State, which was nicknamed Linebacker U at that time. I could conceivably have been a Nittany Lion linebacker on Penn State's national championship team of 1986. But I turned down the offer of a scholarship in a tough final phone call to Paterno.

I had dreamed, like any child, of playing football for the New York Giants or New York Jets in the Meadowlands at the stadium that was just twenty minutes from my home.

That dream didn't seem so far-fetched when top football universities came calling. At least one hundred made serious inquiries. We got letters at home every day, and more came to school. I had my pick of some great schools. Pittsburgh, Boston College, and West Virginia were among them. Believe me, it's pretty heady stuff when heavyweight college coaches like Faust, Paterno, Jack Bicknell of Boston College, and Foge Fazio of Pitt show up at your high school to see you. Many of the coaches wanted to be seen, so they'd make a big show of walking the halls and introducing themselves. That was part of the player seduction.

I had never had so much attention. Neither had the school, I've been told. Many of my former educators still think I received the most attention of any athlete ever at the high school. That's pretty subjective, but I certainly was the first to earn a football scholarship to Notre Dame, the most famous football university in the nation.

Penn State was probably the most famous school from the east. It also has a strong engineering program. That was the field I was most interested in then, so I'd have to say that would have been my next obvious choice. The recruiting process was fun. It was cool to get the attention and visit places I'd never been before.

The visits were a whirlwind of activities, with games and parties to attend. They were fun times, for sure, but I never succumbed to the pressure of booze and other things in high school. The visits made Notre Dame look even better. Something major that bothered me about going to Penn State was the large number of linebackers there already—and more committing to go there. I wanted to play right away. The Nittany Lions played a rugged, stay-in-the-system, side-to-side style.

My main asset was speed in getting to the ball—the quarterback or the ballcarrier—or sealing off the corners. Anyway, my recruiting visit just didn't click at Penn State. It seemed like the players were trying to talk me out of coming there at the same time as the coaches were putting on the hard sell, offering me a scholarship and telling me I could play a lot as a linebacker in my sophomore year. I wanted to play now.

Several of the Nittany Lion players repeated a refrain: "There are too many linebackers here already. I heard they were going to make you a wide receiver or running back." Whether those rumors were true or not didn't really matter.

At Pitt, the team seemed like it was full of cliques when I visited there. The offense and defense didn't hang together. There was so much tension between them. I thought that was strange. It was important to me for my team to be bonded like family. The common goal is winning the game, so everyone has to play their parts. I didn't feel wanted anywhere else like I did at Notre Dame.

During my visit, all-American running back Allen Pinkett showed me around campus. He showed me the basements in all the dorms. That was where all the parties were, and we did have a good time as we visited some of them. The party scene was a common theme on recruiting visits at all the universities. But Allen didn't focus on the fun times. He spoke more about academia than football, about having a university family for life.

I far more enjoyed being in a team family. That kind of thing isn't easy for an eighteen-year-old to decipher. It's just a gut feeling. Penn State had an amazing program and obviously one of the best coaches in the history of the game. But it just didn't fit.

The downfall of Paterno and the program has been distressing to read about. We deal with child abuse situations on a daily basis at Wernle. It was so unfortunate and unbelievable to hear about the scandal involving former coach Jerry Sandusky that apparently reached back into my playing days. Heck, Sandusky was the defensive coordinator for every year when I could have played for the Nittany Lions if I had chosen to accept a scholarship there. Who could have guessed the problems that would devastate Penn State and Paterno, possibly even contributing to his death early in 2012?

Maybe it was God's intervention that I went to Notre Dame.

Universities started showing interest in me as a football player after my coach, Larry Coppola, sent a tape of a game or two during my junior season. I didn't know he was doing that. During one game, I had three sacks and two fumble recoveries. And I also rushed for a couple of touchdowns. I normally averaged about fifteen tackles per game in high school.

Again, it wasn't like today, where thousands of high schoolers are primping for the cameras, and their schools have high-tech video departments. ESPN's stable of channels broadcasts several high school games every week in the fall now, it seems. We didn't even watch much tape of the games we played, much less of our upcoming opponents.

Coach Coppola, who was also my world history teacher, made many things happen for me. He was truly committed to me and was an inspiration and a fatherly figure.

I didn't see myself as a star athlete or playing football at a prestigious place such as Notre Dame. He saw something in me and worked endlessly to gain the attention of colleges around the country. Coach Coppola made my case as a top recruit.

If Larry didn't take the time to make the tape and send it to the right places, I probably wouldn't have gotten noticed. I had an interest in attending college, but I was very naive about the process of getting there.

Nobody could really stop my combination of speed, strength, and football instincts. That had been the pattern since Pop Warner football, but everything seemed to come into place that junior season when notice came to me like never before.

My statistics were phenomenal as I wore the no. 8 jersey of Hillside High, including making more than twenty sacks of the quarterback and many touchdowns as a running back. We had a great team.

That season set the stage for me to be named to the Adidas All-American Team in football for the next season. I participated in elite camps. Those combinations were what sent my notice over the top.

Once you got on the radar screen, there were team scouts, mainly volunteers, who would come to watch you play. Major football-playing teams have thousands of alumni who are ready to help in any way to continue their football successes. Irish followers would also approach me to say hi after games. They were making the family sell. Word of mouth was just as important then as game tapes.

Once Notre Dame saw my grades improve, Gerry Faust visited me several times. The academic board must accept you at Notre Dame before the coaches can give you an offer. A lot goes on before you can hear the words "We want to offer you a scholarship." Gerry actually spent more time with Mom and Dad than with me. The other coaches all visited mainly with me.

Gerry really had a personality. He's the kind of guy who never met a stranger and was spiritual. He would give you the shirt off his back. He was a true representative of the institution. You knew he was your best friend. You loved the guy. He had a knack, I think, because he spent so much time in high schools.

Gerry's high school program in Cincinnati was known as the most successful in the country before he went to Notre Dame. Gerry knew the way to a recruit's heart ran through his home. His impact on my life, from recruiting to now, is so significant that I have written a whole chapter about him.

To tell you the absolute truth, signing day was kind of a letdown. I thought there would be a big hoopla, but it was a quiet signing with an assistant coach from Notre Dame. The important stuff, the decision, had already been made. The recruitment process proved I was wanted, but I needed to prove something to myself before I stepped foot in Notre Dame. I was skinny and very insecure about my weight.

The main question I had was, Am I really good enough to excel in college football?

Yes, I could get to the quarterback coming off corners as fast as anyone in high school, and it was a breeze. It was normal for me. I was pretty humble about it. One time, I jumped over a lineman and grabbed the ball as the quarterback was ready to throw. I literally grabbed it and ran for a touchdown.

An all-star football game in the summer before heading to South Bend helped prove to me that I had something special. I made an interception, forced a fumble, and had two sacks by halftime for the

East team. I made an open-field tackle on a wide receiver. I overheard the radio announcer say, "The MVP at this point is Flash Gordon."

Maybe I am pretty good, I remember thinking then. It was such a confidence builder. It was the ability for me to reaffirm who I was.

It gave me the credibility that I was looking for as a football player heading toward my freshman year at Notre Dame. Thankfully, the university also forced me to turn my focus toward academics. In the long run, that is the biggest credibility you can have. The bright lights can go out at any minute for athletes, but college degrees can light up your life forever.

CHAPTER 5

Freshman Survival

I WAS READY to battle in the big-time atmosphere at Notre Dame as a football player.

My boxing-champion brother, Victor, had shown me the way to handle the bright lights and the adoring crowds. But I was woefully unprepared for another battle: the academic rigors of the University of Notre Dame.

I needed to take the fighting part of the Irish into the classroom. In order to succeed on the football field, I had to keep up with an academic pace unlike anything I'd ever experienced. It took major adjustments just to make it through the first year.

The first disappointment hit me quickly. Coaches decided to redshirt me because of a lingering ankle injury. That meant I was designated to the practice squad and couldn't play in any games.

Academic disappointment was another story, certainly a more serious one. The expectations on the campus were shockingly challenging at first. I was already overwhelmed and certainly downcast because I couldn't play in games. Since I had a bit more free time than other players, it was too easy to find a party, to hang out with fun people, and to slack off on my classes. The result after the first semester was that I came perilously close to getting kicked out. My grade point average was lower than a 2.0.

Shortly after returning for the second semester, I received a notice of academic probation in my mailbox at school. It was a shock. I thought I'd have a year to prove myself. I had to immensely improve my grades, or the school would send me home. I remember pondering whether I should just go back to New Jersey anyway. The notice shook me up and my parents too. Unbeknownst to me, they were sent the probation notice, which certainly told them that I had goofed off too much in a dreadful first semester. Both called to say, "What's going on, Darrell? You can do a lot better than that!" I remember my dad saying, "That's not you. You have many gifts, so use them."

I remember lying awake in bed many times in the wee hours of the morning. (That's unusual because I usually nod off within minutes of lying down.) I couldn't sleep because I knew I couldn't let my family down. I had pride to uphold for my family and my hometown. I was going to become the first college graduate in my immediate family.

My coaches were obviously concerned about my first-semester grades too. It helped so much that they were supportive and that they didn't panic. They set me up with tutoring help and study groups, but I basically had to find it within myself to succeed. The warning served its purpose. It awakened the fighting spirit within me.

Starting with the spring semester, I made the changes necessary to succeed academically as well as athletically. I quickly devised a disciplined plan. The central point was nightly treks to the library. It became my second room as I drove myself to keep up and succeed in my classes. Every night, I arrived at the same time and used the same room. I left when it closed. A librarian would lock the door behind me and say, "See you tomorrow, Flash." Those kind words rang louder than any applause I received for making a tackle for the Irish.

Another Irish player who had received a similar probation notice went with me a lot too. And we worked together. We both did what we needed to do. I learned two vital things through that probation process: I could do the work, and I belonged at a school like Notre Dame. That was the beginning of a mission: nobody could stop me, except me. What I lacked in an educational background, I made up in determination and the ability to learn from coaches, teachers, and mentors.

My upbringing, athletic talents, and commitment put me in a position to make dramatic changes. I am not going to mislead you, though. Those changes didn't come without a lot of angst, self-doubts, and sleepless nights. Those changes didn't come without foregoing good times and even leaving some friends behind.

Those changes set the foundation for everything in my life today. Nothing I have accomplished would have been possible without accepting more challenges and making more changes to prosper at Notre Dame. I had no idea how high I could climb until I stepped on that campus. I had to take some steps back before I could step forward. The situation was a parallel to what I had faced in high school. But it was a quantum leap to survive there as a student compared to high school.

My personality won't allow me just to survive at something. I want to thrive. I want to finish first and to have big goals and big achievements.

That inner motivation drove me every day to be the best in the weight room and on the practice field. It meant I could learn to compete with the best in the Notre Dame classroom. The young adults who come to Notre Dame are generally the best of the best. They are the leaders, the valedictorians, and the magna cum laudes in their senior classes at high school.

Even in recent times, as I have sat on the alumni board and the Monogram Club board, the word is shared from admissions folks that being ranked in the top of your high school class doesn't guarantee admittance. In fact, only about 29 percent of applicants get in. The Scholastic Aptitude Test scores of those who are admitted are stratospheric in comparison to most students.

Athletes such as me quickly realize what they are competing against. When an athlete hits an environment like that—and I don't think I was even in the top 50 of my senior class—you have to have immense confidence in yourself. You have to be willing to push yourself harder mentally and physically.

You have less time to work at being a good student than most ordinary undergraduates. You have less time to sleep and less time for a social life. Most students have from noon to midnight to study if they load up on morning classes like athletes do. But because of practices and other preparations that run from 2:00 PM to 8:00 PM every day, the players have only from 8:00 PM to midnight to study during the season, which covers the complete fall semester and about half of the spring. There is little time to adjust because football is played in their first semester on campus. Athletes can simply get overwhelmed. But the pace forces you to manage your life. Most players find a way.

As a beginning college student, you can be very much alone until you start making decisions, putting your priorities in order. I had to constantly tell myself, "I am going to graduate from the University of Notre Dame. I am going to play, if not start, for the Irish. I am going to have a social life. My management skills better be second to none."

I had from January to late April to get my grades up. That went by very quickly.

I can remember watching other students throwing Frisbees on the quad as the weather warmed in spring. But I had to bypass the flowers and the good times. Letting up would be treacherous.

Notre Dame has proven year after year that athletes can compete at high levels. They are competitive. They can find a way to get it done. In fact, Notre Dame athletes carry a higher GPA than traditional students. Some other programs have trouble graduating a fourth of their football players. A probation notice probably isn't so jarring at those kinds of colleges.

But Notre Dame has always graduated about 98 percent of its players (usually at the top of the country). I simply couldn't allow myself to be in the minority of 2 percent. Academics and athletics are on parallel paths toward excellence at Notre Dame. Outside of the adulation from fans, athletes aren't really treated any different than any other students. There were no athletic dorms or separate dining halls. Athletes are forced to mingle.

The question I started asking myself after my first-semester setback was, Could I compete at Notre Dame after going through a public school? That's a hard question. So many players from tough backgrounds haven't been taught the discipline needed to excel in academics. My high school actually did a great job, though. Many students went on to Ivy League schools.

My struggles weren't unfamiliar to many athletes that come out of urban high schools in one respect. The academic preparation isn't rigorous enough. There could be many other factors, of course. Among them, their home life is in shambles, they lack mentors, or they simply don't have the internal drive to overcome barriers.

I am convinced that the perseverance of that first year directly led to the three major achievements that happened to me at Notre Dame. I was handed a bachelor's degree in business and economics in May of 1988, played as a starter for the Irish as they won a national title under Coach Lou Holtz in January 1989, and then earned my graduate degree in administration in August of 1989.

In a way, I was just needing a chance.

I think it bears bringing up the movie *Rudy*, which bears that theme. That movie is by far my favorite. It was a dream for thousands of young players every year to play for the Irish. The true story of *Rudy* involves a tenacious and dyslexic student named Rudy Ruettiger, who was too small and not talented enough to play football for Notre Dame in the 1970s. He just wanted a chance.

He prodded coaches for months and eventually found a way to make the practice team. He went all out on the practice field, something that we share in common. He reveled in wearing an Irish practice uniform, whether it was during two-a-day practices in ninety-degree weather or late-season practices on an icy field. Finally, Coach Dan Devine allowed him to suit up for a game in the last game of his senior season. He participated in two plays as a five feet five, 165-pound defensive end. His sack of the quarterback on the second play stands as memorably to some Notre Dame fans as the Irish's eleven national titles.

His Notre Dame story is an inspiration for other reasons too. He was older than most students because he had served in the navy and worked for two years before starting college. He was rejected three times before finally getting accepted into Notre Dame.

His story epitomizes that working hard and following your dreams can take you anywhere. His story is spiritual in a sense, just as is the whole campus atmosphere. The powerful presence of Christ was evident on every corner.

Notre Dame sets the example by surrounding students with pastoral support. Beautiful chapels are situated in most buildings, offering places for prayer and quiet contemplation. Christ-centered icons are everywhere: beautiful crosses, paintings, and stained glass windows. The buildings are rich and exquisite with tradition: the Basilica of the Sacred Heart, Log Chapel, the Golden Dome of the main administration building.

My campus relationships have been infused with spirituality, from classmates to teammates, from pastors to professors, from janitors to librarians.

The football team prays before every home game at the Grotto of the Lady of Lourdes, and then walks to the stadium hand in hand. The famed Touchdown Jesus mural stands guard just outside the Notre Dame Stadium.

But the spirituality is much deeper and everlasting than that. The dormitories there each have a priest and a chapel. The dorms also have wonderful housekeepers who often double as confidants, religious advisers, and surrogate moms.

At Notre Dame, the housekeepers cleaned your room and did your laundry. To say they knew your dirty laundry was not an exaggeration. That idea is against most concepts of college life as the time students learn to take care of themselves. But the Notre Dame style is for students to focus entirely on the educational and spiritual experience while they are there.

My roommate, Reggie Ward, and I knew we had to be on good behavior because the housekeeper could enter at any time. They were truly like surrogate moms. It was just amazing. We respected them. We loved them. We didn't want to disappoint them.

The one I remembered the most was nicknamed Skip. She called me Flash and always had a smile on her face. It was a job and a commitment for them. Their service and love taught us to always consider how we treat all people—to always respect others as well as ourselves. The Golden Rule was always evident under the Golden Dome: "Do unto others as you'd have them do unto you."

My dormitory, Alumni Hall, had two priests that resided there—Father E. William Beauchamp and Father George. Father Beauchamp was a vice president at Notre Dame. In fact, at the same time as living in a small apartment, he was chairman of Notre Dame's Faculty Board in Control of Athletics, overseeing twenty-two varsity, forty-seven intramural, and nine club sports. He is now president of the University of Portland. "Everyone here is involved in the one mission of the university, to educate our students," he said once about Notre Dame in a published interview. His overall mission and message was that athletes are students first at Notre Dame.

Father George is still there in his one-bedroom apartment with a den. Everything in there is cherrywood, high quality. I still drop by to visit him. Year after year, he imparts his wisdom on new waves of young men. Father George didn't work a forty-hour week. He was on call every minute of every day. The dorm was his home, and we were his children. The door to his apartment was usually wide open. He held us accountable. If he had to address anyone in disciplinary fashion, I didn't see it. The door would be closed then, and he'd handle it in a private way. We all knew that Father George went to bed about 3:00 AM and that it would be most polite if we didn't knock on his door before 11:00 AM. He positioned himself where he needed to be.

He knew he needed to spend his time with students in the wee hours of the morning, when some people are most troubled, when they needed someone to talk to, to crack a joke with. Father George was the pastor of your personal church. He would lead services and hear confessions.

Having a chapel there was amazing. I would just sit in there each night for a while. The chapel and Father George were an amazing resource for me during my first-year struggles. I'd see others in the chapel, too, and wonder, What were they going through?

Notre Dame gets it about support in life: you provide an environment to help students excel no matter what they are pursuing in life, whether you are an athlete, an arts major, an architectural student, or anything in between. It's a campus, a common bond, a character builder, and an icon of commitment. Notre Dame offers all its students and alumni a foundation for success and moral support for life. I know it will always be there for me any time I need it.

CHAPTER 6

Gerry's Campus

GERRY FAUST IS God's goodwill ambassador for football. He is a humble beacon of everything good about the game. I thank God that he was the coach who picked me and enticed me to play at Notre Dame. My world changed from the moment Coach Faust called to offer me a scholarship. Little did I realize the amount of time he put into learning about me. Gerry is a fine football coach and a fabulous man. He epitomizes the meaning of family.

He is the kind of principled guy who said no to the nation's top running back recruit one year because the young man swore at his mother because she "messed" with his stereo by turning down the volume. "Don't talk to your mom like that!" Gerry yelled over the music. "You apologize to your mother and give her a kiss." Moments later, Gerry shocked the recruit by saying, "You go somewhere else to school. If you treat your mother like that, you can't be a part of our family."

That's why good coaches go into homes. Gerry loved what he found in my home. Truth be told, his scholarship offer was really to my mother and father, and they accepted for me. There was no way I was going to let them down.

Like other successful coaches, Gerry knew the way to a recruit's heart ran through his home. In my case, it was through my mom's kitchen and my dad's garage. But he took that to a whole other level. One day, during recruiting season (midway through my senior year), I came home from school and found Gerry sitting at our kitchen table, eating my mother's spaghetti and talking to her like they were best buddies.

I remember selfishly thinking, *Why's he talking to my mom? I'm the football player he wants.* But he was the smart one. For one, we all agree that my mom's food was great. If there was any doubt where I was leaning, it was sealed when my mom said she thought Notre Dame would be a great fit. Her gut trusted Gerry.

So did my dad's. Gerry visited him at his shop. Amazingly, those visits are still clear in Gerry's memory. "Our minds were made up after we visited that we wanted you at Notre Dame," he said by phone from his home in Ohio.

He remembers the chats and the pasta and the cleanliness of my dad's shop. "They were the nicest people. Your mom and dad were tremendous people," Gerry recalls. "We just knew you were a great kid, and you would be great for our program. When you had parents like you had, we just couldn't lose with you."

Gerry believes that young men are recruited to be a part of a football family. That meant character counted. So did grades. "We wanted to make sure they came from an environment where family came first. I always took the time to get to know the families, and I never took a player that didn't come from a good family environment," Gerry said.

He recruited the top classes year after year. Many players came from great single-parent households. Some were brought up by grandparents. Some came from broken families, such as mine. But all families have a quality that's concrete and noticeable.

Gerry wanted to know all about me. He wanted to impress upon my parents that I would be treated like family at Notre Dame. "A team should be a family," he said. "When you are, you work together." Gerry's style meant that my mom and dad knew before I did that Notre Dame was the right place for me. The school's qualities, as enunciated through Gerry, were exactly what they stood for.

Gerry promised something that other recruiters didn't: I'd graduate and be prepared to move forward through life after football.

He also promised something that other schools didn't: a network that would help gain jobs throughout the process. They used the network well with CEOs. I spent the summer on Wall Street after my second year at Notre Dame.

The program would even help secure jobs for you during summer before you came. You shared your interests, and they'd find people who specialized in that area. They made sure all the freshmen had jobs. My first job was working as a painter at the Meadowlands, where I dreamed of playing football after my college career. I was excited about having so many choices. Neither one turned out long-term, though. I never had the chance to become an NFL star, and I was never a good painter. One reason was, I quickly learned that I was scared of heights. The highest I'd ever been before was climbing up a few stories in an apartment building. I hadn't climbed anything else except a tree.

Gerry explains that he had a quick three-step process for recruiting a student-athlete for the Irish. Two of the steps were student oriented. He had to be academically sound and be capable of earning a university degree. The third ingredient was being a high-level, high-class athlete. "You had all those things," Gerry said. "We checked you out!"

The focus on academics made my parents see the wisdom of going to Notre Dame. My mom knew this was the kind of opportunity she and my father had dreamed about as they were leaving South Carolina. She had graduated from high school, but her opportunities just weren't there for any further education after she became a mother of five.

In New Jersey, she worked long hours in a linen factory for many years before she had children and worked again afterward. She did a great job with the resources she had. But money was always an issue. There was never enough. There were challenges on occasions.

Mom knew that education was the highway from New Jersey to new frontiers for me.

Coming to Notre Dame certainly was a new frontier. It was the Old West in my mind as well as a dream come true. I remember driving there the first time. Indiana was so foreign to me. Soon, it would be my home.

I'd live in dorms just like every other student. I wouldn't be treated like a saint. There would be nothing special about me on campus. Every student is inherently special there because of the university's selection process. If you are invited in, you already have what they think you need to succeed.

Gerry took great care in the vetting process. The first step was finding out that I was a good player. "Our coach who recruited that area found you. We looked at film and knew right then that you were going to be an outstanding player."

My high school head coach, Larry Coppola, played a critical role by getting tapes out to the coaches and scouts and extolling my character. "Your coach was outstanding that way," Gerry recalls. "I did the same thing when I was a high school coach."

Gerry knows about being an effective high school coach. He was 178-23-2 and won four national championships at Moeller High in Cincinnati, Ohio. He led Moeller to seven undefeated seasons.

The next step after identifying a potential recruit "is to find out what kind of person he is," Gerry said about his process.

That included visiting a potential player's daily environment. "You see people at school, see his family," Gerry said. "I'd go around in hallways and ask, How is this guy? I'd always find out a lot. In your case, you were well liked by everybody. Our analysis was that we were getting a first-class player and, more importantly, a first-class young man."

Gerry loved his players before they ever hit campus. "I don't think we had a bad kid," he remembers. "That's what makes Notre Dame so unique."

All the players came to love Gerry. He was caring. He was eternally optimistic. He was motivational. He gave players wide liberties. He was simply a great guy.

It turned out, though, that he simply wasn't the right fit for winning big in South Bend. A great thing about that is Gerry knew it then and isn't ashamed to admit it now. The Irish never got on a major roll in his five seasons—he was 30-26-1—and he resigned before the Irish ended at 5–6 in 1985. His best record was 7–5, accomplished in 1983 and 1984.

In retrospect, I believe Gerry was such a wonderful man that he wasn't tough enough on his players. Many of the stars and should-be leaders would bail out on practices with excuses about injuries or other minor issues. Team and individual discipline were issues.

Gerry's tenure started with great optimism. He was the most well-known high school football coach in history when he came to the most celebrated college program. It was his dream job. The fans hoped he'd deliver dozens of big wins and more national championships. But they never happened. Gerry deserves a lot of respect for what he did do. He helped set the stage for a championship three seasons after he left. Several of his recruits played major roles in that title.

Lou Holtz, the coach who followed him, always gave Gerry rightful respect.

"He let me live the dream," Gerry said about Notre Dame leader Father Joyce. "But I stepped down because I knew these young men deserved better. When they won the national championship, I was so proud of those kids and Coach Holtz."

Gerry continues to be a great friend and inspiration, always only a phone call away. Let me give you a recent example. He called to say a former Irish player could really use some financial and moral support. The former star player needed to find a job in the Midwest. I felt honored to be approached. Of course, I would help the best I could. The Irish family doesn't turn away from former players (no matter what the sport). It's simply what you are supposed to do. It's a reflection of what you are.

I realized that this player needed to make major changes in his life, that it could be hard. I also realized that I wouldn't just offer my hard-earned money. Financial issues are almost always symptomatic of deeper personal problems. The former player needed a plan, support, and follow-through. I would be there to help him, and so would dozens of other former Irish players and fans.

Football players are geared up to win games and championships. That will never go away. But victories only last a short while. Gerry always preached that, and so did Coach Holtz. "It's more important to win the hearts of football players," Gerry said. "The real win is what they do afterward. I recruited 150 players, and only two did not graduate. Not one of them has ever dishonored themselves or the university. They are all my heroes. I'm so proud of them."

My good friend Allen Pinkett starred as a running back while playing for Gerry. He concurs about the everlasting examples of goodness that Gerry brought to the game. "It really wasn't fair that Gerry didn't win enough at Notre Dame," Pinkett said. "He lived the role and loved everything about it. Maybe he loved it too much."

Gerry has no regrets. That's the way things go in life. "I've been blessed," he said. "Why would the good Lord give me an opportunity like that and it not work out? It was meant to work out that way."

That is a cornerstone of Gerry's message when he speaks to people. It's more than ironic that my college coaches and I have followed the same path to motivational speaking. We all have different messages, but the roots are the same: love, respect, excellence, hard work, and change. "I've been at the top and the bottom," Gerry said. People listen more closely to him, he believes, because he's been at both spectrums.

You can get through anything with three simple things: faith, family, and friends.

CHAPTER 7

Learning to Win the Lou Way

TRUST. LOVE. COMMITMENT. Those words were a mission as we marched toward glory in the 1988 season. Every Irish player from that season carried a daily reminder of the three words. They are imprinted on our championship rings. They were the daily pronouncements of our teacher and preacher, Coach Lou Holtz.

Trust, love, commitment are more than words. They are a vision and a mission for success throughout life. I love Lou for leading us to greatness on the Irish, for leading me. But I couldn't say that was the case as I sat in his office in the winter of 1988 and heard him tell me to get lost. That's right. He told me to leave the Irish football team.

We had been embarrassed in the Cotton Bowl just weeks before. And he had decided to clean house of all the incoming seniors. He didn't think that we were focusing and playing hard enough to help the Irish grow into a champion. He didn't think that we were committed enough, could sacrifice enough.

Several players left. Thankfully, though, I convinced Lou to let me prove him wrong in spring practice. If Lou had prevailed, I would have been watching the Irish play on television that fall instead of playing as linebacker. I would never have been pictured with Ronald Reagan for a title celebration during his final day as president in January 1989. I would never have been invited to play in the Hula Bowl along with players such as Deion Sanders, Troy Aikman, Andre Rison, and Derrick Thomas, all who went on to become major stars in the NFL.

I probably would have left campus after earning my bachelor's degree and missed getting a graduate degree and many other glorious things that have taken place since then. Instead, the situation led to one of my greatest life lessons: loving someone and asking them to leave isn't always a contradiction. It can be a fatherly test. It can light a fire that makes you reach for the best. Being asked to leave can open a door that allows you to focus and work so that you can stay forever.

Lou knew what he was doing. His goodbye moves chased away some players who probably weren't going to help him. Conversely, those seniors who persevered would be a hungry, hardworking, title-seeking bunch. It certainly fed my hunger. I remember thinking, *I am not going out like that.* It's pushed me to perform at a consistently higher level.

Lou was far more than a coach. He was masterful at getting into the minds of young players and getting them to play at peak performance. Everything in coaching revolved around two simple goals for Lou: win games and educate students. His players were expected to earn titles and college degrees and then move on to a lifetime of work that benefited people.

He led so well at Notre Dame that his name stands with Knute Rockne, Frank Leahy, and Ara Parshegian as the best coaches in the history of Irish football. In fact, Lou's only second to Knute in victories: 100 to 105. Ara had 95, and Frank 87.

Lou's qualities help make him one of the best ever at his other crafts: giving speeches, writing books, and being an ESPN analyst for college football. Out of the limelight, he also exemplifies what is right and what's respectful in life.

Looking back, it was respect that kept me on the team. Lou and the other coaches knew I worked as hard as anyone in the weight room and on the practice field.

But Lou wanted more. I was weeks away from graduating with my undergraduate degree in economics and business, so I'm not certain if I would have—or could have—stuck around for my final football season, in which I worked toward a graduate degree in administration. Without that graduate degree, I doubt I would ever have attended law school.

Thankfully, another of Lou's traits came into play when he delivered the "don't come back" message. He listened to my protests and gave me the room (with a short rope) to stay on the team. Essentially, I was told, "Don't screw up." I was so inspired in spring practice that I went full tilt on every play. The result was that I had the best spring during my time at South Bend. I was considered a starter going into the championship season.

Lou's reasons for pushing out some older players weren't personal. He was making tough decisions after an embarrassing 35–10 loss to Texas A&M in the Cotton Bowl. Led by Heisman Trophy winner Tim Brown, we actually led that game 7–0 and 10–3 before collapsing. We were handcuffed by four turnovers at critical times, and our defense allowed nearly three hundred yards rushing.

We finished 8–4 in Notre Dame's one hundredth season of football, but that wasn't nearly good enough. We weren't playing our best at the end of the season after a month of practicing.

Lou cared about every player, but his job was to build a champion. He needed to make changes because he hadn't seen the growth in the Irish that he wanted after two seasons as coach. He felt there were some lackadaisical efforts from the upcoming seniors. We were athletic, but we lacked leadership. Lou needed seniors who would sacrifice and lead.

The defense especially was considered to be inconsistent. In fact, there were numerous published stories coming into the championship season that the defense was our weakest link. Lou wanted to forge ahead with players he'd recruited to mirror his vision.

Believing that Lou's side of the story is also essential, I also am offering his insights below:

"We had a good team. We were making progress. They were good people, good players. I decided the most important thing was there wasn't a changed attitude yet. They didn't have the passion I wanted. It wasn't the players' faults. I sat down with many players, including you, Flash, and said, 'It's best you move on. I just don't want you to come back.' You begged me to give you a chance. You'd adjust, buy in. But I was adamant you weren't coming back."

No one has had a bigger effect on my life than Coach Holtz after he stepped into lead the Irish in 1986. I was going into my junior season and anticipated being a starter at linebacker by default because of experience. Boy, was that a flawed presumption.

Lou isn't afraid to make any change needed to achieve his goal. That's a sign of a great leader, whether it's in football, business, or daily life. He demands respect. He did exactly that with the first words he said after being introduced to the complete team at Notre Dame. "Get your foot off the stage. Sit up," he told a key player who sat in the front row with his feet casually up on the stage of the tight room. I was shocked. The whole room grew quiet. It was common for a player to do that until then. But a new sheriff was in town. He kicked at the player's feet and asked how long he'd played football. The basic premise was that if he wanted to continue playing at Notre Dame, respect would be mandatory. Lou vividly remembers the scene:

"It's that simple. I had a vision where I wanted to take the program. If you aren't going to buy in, it won't work."

Part of buying in included "Keep your feet on the ground, eyes on me and communicate." Coach Holtz continued, "I wanted to be competitive, have a contender every year. I wanted the players to reflect values of togetherness, passion, excellence. From that time on, they sat up. That's the only way it should be."

Lou's action has become the stuff of legends. Chris Zorich, an all-American lineman who was in Holtz's first recruiting class at Notre Dame, said players talked about it in mystical terms all during his time there. "You're kidding. You were there. It's true." Zorich laughed recently. "We'd always heard about that."

Zorich said players loved Holtz and feared him. We agree on that. He forced us to pay attention to detail, to show respect, and to act like a champion. We learned by watching Lou speak and interact with players on and off the field. He had a way of gaining your attention and making you think.

Soon after taking over the Irish, Lou delivered one of the most valuable lessons in my life. I got a call in my dorm room from his personal assistant. Lou wanted to meet with me in his office. I thought we'd chat about where I fit into his plans, maybe get a pat on the back and a motivational push with two starters graduating.

Selfishly and naively, I thought perhaps he'd share with me about what he thought of my skills, saying something like "I saw you on film and you have great abilities. You have a great future here."

The chat took a completely different direction. It was more than about football. His first question caught me off guard: "Mr. Gordon, what distinguishes you from anyone else at this institution?" Lou has a unique way of drawing out his words, so it sounded more like "innnstituuutionnnn."

I answered that I was a potential all-American and NFL star. That's not what he was looking for. He repeated the question time and again as I fumbled with answers, trying to figure out where he was going. Finally, he said what should distinguish me is character.

He pointed out that football players weren't any better than anyone else at Notre Dame. The whole university needed to be a team. Lou's campus included everybody who was focused on success: the priests and professors, the librarians and the janitors, the ticket takers and the tailgaters.

He often says that football lasts just four years, but a career is at least forty. He was getting us ready to win at our jobs, as spouses, as parents, as neighbors.

Just after coming in, he had T-shirts produced that showed the word *TEAM* in huge letters and *ME* in tiny letters. There is no me in team.

"I never felt I coached football. It was a subject matter. I taught life," Coach Holtz said. He also stressed the importance of being committed: "Never lose the trust of people you work for. Are you committed to excellence? How much sacrifice are you willing to make [for example, can you give up drinking and carousing to study and work out more]? Everybody wants to win. The question is, Do you care about the team, what's best for the team?"

I left that initial meeting and thought about his question again and again. *What distinguishes you from anyone else at this institution?* It ran through my mind constantly as I decided to attend graduate and law schools. It runs through my mind all the time in my work leading Wernle Youth & Family Treatment Center. Any campus, any business, any institution must work as a team with a clear vision of its goals.

The focus has to be on these: What are we doing here? What are the missions?

For us at Wernle, it's helping troubled young boys and girls find the tools to have better lives. It's modeling respect, compassion, and professionalism, the same as Coach Holtz constantly modeled. Do the right thing. Do the best you can. Show you care.

"Those apply everywhere," Coach Holtz said. "You have to generate trust and be committed to excellence. Caring about one another builds that."

Coach and I shared in an amazing experience off the field during our championship season—one that's he's written about in his books.

Things went well for me for several games. Then my playing time drastically diminished as a younger player played more and more at outside linebacker. I didn't play in the historic 31–30 victory over Miami in what many people consider a top10 game ever in college football. The Hurricanes were ranked no. 1 and had won thirty-six consecutive regular-season games. We were ranked no. 2. I remember thinking, *You're telling me I'm not good enough to get on this field?*

It was hard to celebrate, I'll admit, because I didn't contribute to the victory. There was no use to complain about it during the games or let up at practice. Acting up wasn't my style. But it hurt my psyche and my confidence. I thought I wasn't being treated fairly. I imagine Lou dealt with hundreds and hundreds of players expressing the same dismay during his career.

But he really listened to me when I dropped into his office to vent about it. I laid out my reasoning for regaining my starting job. He asked some questions and dismissed me. It was very respectful. Lou made no promises.

He checked with other coaches, including Defensive Coordinator Barry Alvarez, and looked at how I had graded out during practices and games. I always went full tilt during both of them, even if I had to tackle a star player hard in practice.

That happened at times. If I weren't going to start in the coming week, I'd practice with the second team, which normally lined up against the first team. I felt like I wanted to prove myself on every play, to give 100 percent. That's just the way I played. It drew notice. Lou informed me that I deserved to play more, and he then helped make that happen.

That's a class act. He is forceful, but fair-minded. I'm certain those attributes helped us become a championship team and helped Lou deservedly win several honors as coach of the year for that season. I am honored that Lou wrote that I was one of his top defenders the last five games of that title season and one of the best in the 34–21 Fiesta Bowl victory over no. 3 West Virginia that earned Notre Dame its eleventh national title.

"You handled it the right way," Coach Holtz said. "You didn't bitch and moan. You came to us. You're positive, upbeat. There's nobody I have more respect for than you, Flash Gordon, because of your adjustment and how you handled the situation. I told you, 'Flash, I think you have a point.' You played brilliantly after that. You were an integral part of our team, a leader."

Lou is a charismatic and humorous speaker—one of the most popular and respected in the world. He has been a great help for me in my work at Wernle and my work as a national motivational speaker. Just watching him speak is amazing. He finds a way to gather energy and make every talk special. He practices his craft. He's so motivational.

He gave me a great boost of motivation a few years ago in my quest to be a better speaker. He flew into Indianapolis and met with me for about three hours at a restaurant on a Saturday night. He offered lots of on-point advice about becoming better and also about navigating in the industry. I am so thankful that he offered so much time.

It's imperative that people build their networks if they want to make the changes that are essential in today's high-tech, fast-paced, cost-conscious world. One of the great things about Notre Dame is that the whole campus atmosphere encourages networking. Life is about meeting people and learning from their strengths. So many of my friends came from that experience.

Frank Eck became a great mentor, his son a great friend. I stay in close contact with men I played with, such as Zorich, Reggie Brooks, Tim Brown, and Frank Stams. Zorich, Stams and I were together again recently when about fifty men played on the field of their dreams after a fantasy camp that was led by real Irish assistant coaches. It was a wonderful reminder of the spirit of Notre Dame. The men were from around the country and ranged in age from twenties to sixties. They had used vacation time and paid thousands of dollars to head to the campus in South Bend, to do drills on the same practice field as the Irish, to play in Notre Dame Stadium, and to be coached by real Irish assistants. Those memories will last a lifetime, just as mine have for Irish football.

I know that Lou will always be there for me as a life coach and a friend. He's practical with his advice. He's a major reason I have found successes and aspire to so many more. He's a major reason why I am not afraid to make major changes and want to help others learn to do the same.

Leaders sometimes have to say, "I'm not here to be loved. I'm here to make you better, make the team better."

You have to be aware that people will disagree. They will fight change. Yet it's necessary. You can demand respect and excellent results while also being fair-minded and compassionate. You can learn to love the people who care enough to push you to higher levels of excellence.

Lou's philosophy carries forward today in my role as CEO on the Wernle campus.

Major changes are sometimes necessary to move forward. And often it doesn't pay to wait. Make an immediate impression. If something is a mess, clean it up. Make the changes you must as a leader. Most importantly, never lose sight of your mission.

Lou was a model of making strategic changes. They certainly left their fingerprints all over the national championship.

"You should welcome change, embrace it," Coach Holtz said. "Make sure you are changing to make your goal. Win and graduate. Everything had to help that."

Coach Holtz showed he was a class act, starting out with his changes by never criticizing the program of Coach Gerry Faust.

But Lou didn't lead the Irish back overnight. We went 5–6 under him, then 8–4, *then* 12–0. This was his dream job, just like it was for Gerry. Lou added players with the speed we needed to compete with the Miamis, Michigans, and USCs—teams that were regularly beating us. He was omnipresent in every part of the program. You never really knew where he'd show up. But he'd be out there at practice, teaching, prodding, and pushing. He'd run wind sprints with us. He'd catch punts and stick his head in to demonstrate a block or a tackle. He once rushed in and knocked over quarterback Tony Rice, who had been goofing off at practice, in a scene made famous by an article in *Time* magazine.

Lou's philosophy was that if practices were tough, the games would be easy. It wasn't an option to slack off. That's what many players will do if you let them at all levels.

No tale describes more the effect of Lou and teamwork on the championship season than what happened the night before the final regular-season game against Southern California. The buzz was nonstop: this was the national championship game.

The Trojans were ranked no. 2, but they were considered the favorite because they were playing at home in the Los Angeles Coliseum. So we could hardly stand to lose two of our offensive stars. But we did, after flanker Ricky Watters and running Tony Brooks arrived a half hour late to dinner the night before the game. There was a team rule that if you were late, you didn't play; they had been warned.

The room was very quiet, with hushed conversations, as we ate a steak-and-shrimp dinner at the hotel. Our whole shot at a title would be determined the next day. Nobody knew where they were or if they had been in an accident. They showed up with bags in their hands and smiles on their faces as if nothing was wrong. They had been shopping and lost track of the time. Lou asked them to go into other rooms. He then gathered the seniors and team captains and said, "I care a lot about your thoughts. I am going to allow you to make the decision." He walked out and left it to us.

Discipline was essential to Lou's regime. He knew he had to follow through and send Watters and Brooks home. We were unanimous after a lot of discussion that they shouldn't play. We cared enough about one another not to compromise. We weren't going to let them dictate that they could do anything they wanted. We delivered the statement for the entire team. A few of the other players were irate when we delivered the decision. "What do you mean?" they cried.

Some newspaper articles questioned the move. But it simply had to be to reiterate the fact that we would be held accountable for the rules. That was a crucial turning point in the team. If they had been allowed to play, all the stars would have known they could break the rules.

But we didn't fold without them. In fact, the opposite happened.

That was the difference in our team: we had a depth of talent. We pulled together as a team like we never did before. The defenders promised that we'd have the biggest game of the season to overcome the loss of offensive firepower. We figured that the Trojans couldn't win if they didn't score. The defense was outstanding. Alvarez gave a great motivational talk: "I promise this defense is going to win this game."

It's worth mentioning that Coach Holtz was forced to do a similar thing while coaching at Arkansas. He kicked off three star members of his team before a bowl game against Oklahoma. The odds grew in the Sooners' favor, and the newspaper stories questioned the merits. The shorthanded Razorbacks easily won the game.

We used the value of positive persuasion to keep telling our senior running back Mark Green that he was going to have a great game. He was the one who would step up with Watters and Brooks gone. He did by scoring two touchdowns as we won 27–10. That meant we had to beat only West Virginia to be the champion.

Our defense stood on its head. I remember the feeling we had when Frank Stams hit USC's star quarterback, Rodney Peete, so hard on a block after an early interception. That's when we really saw we were invincible. Our confidence was amazing. We had bonded into a tight team. How could we be stopped? We couldn't, and we weren't.

"It didn't matter that they were stars," Coach Holtz said. "You don't overlook certain things. All I did was enforce the team's decisions. The more respect with the team, the greater the team. The team won because they were close."

1988 Notre Dame Fighting Irish

First Row, left to right: Chuck Killian, Ted Fitzgerald, Steve Belles, Steve Alaniz, Darrell 'Flash' Gordon, Mark Green, Andy Heck, Ned Bolcar, Wes Pritchett, Frank Stams, Marty Lippincott, Mike Brennan, Pete Graham. **Second Row:** Kurt Zackrison, Steve Roddy, Dave Munger, Brad Alge, Scott Bufton, Ray Dumas, George Streeter, Sean Connor, Tom Gorman, Aaron Robb, Corny Southall, D'Juan Francisco, Bob Satterfield, Pat Eilers, Joe Jarosz, Mike Gatti. **Third Row:** Todd Lyght, Tony Rice, Rod West, Dave Prinzivalli, Bryan Flannery, Mike Crounse, Jeff Alm, Doug Diorio, Reggie Ho, Dan McDevitt, Pete Hartweger, Pat Fallon, Kevin McShane, Mike Stonebreaker, Mike Harazin, Ted McNamara, Mickey Anderson, James Dillard. **Fourth Row:** George Williams, Dave Jandric, Stan Smagala, Dean Brown, Ted Healy, Tim Grunhard, Joe Farrell, Rick Purcell, Marc Dobbins, Mike McLoone, Rich Earley, Braxston Banks, Anthony Johnson, Ryan Mihalko, Jim Kinsherf, Jim Sexton, Billy Hackett, Dave Rosenberg, Chris Zorich. **Fifth Row:** Joe Allen, Bob Dahl, Antwon Lark, Jerry Bodine, Brian Shannon, Norm Balentine, Frank Jacobs, Darryl Wodecki, Donn Grimm, Mike Callan, Kent Graham, Mike Heldt, Winston Sandri, Tim Ryan, Scott Kowalkowski, Greg Davis, Tony Brooks, Ricky Watters, Andre Jones, George Marshall. **Sixth Row:** Jerry Partridge, Larry Tomich, Jay Hayes, Vinny Cerrato, Scott Raridon, Billy Ray Martinov, Jim Strong, John Palermo, Barry Alvarez, Rev. James Riehle, Lou Holtz, Chuck Heater, Pete Cordelli, Joe Moore, Tony Yelovich, George Stewart, George Kelly, Tim Scannell, Mike Bossory, Brian White. **Seventh Row:** Mike Green, Shawn Patrick, Pete Witty (managers) John Whitmer (trainer) Brother John Campbell, Gene O'Neill, Jim Russ, Dwayne Treolo, Kim Garrison, Patty Ferrick, Nicole Lamboley (trainers)

CHAPTER 8

Building a Champion

CHAMPIONSHIPS ARE WON in the mud and blood of the practice fields. They are won in the sweat-stained weight rooms. They are won on two-a-days in 100-degree weather when you are dizzy, lusting after the ice bucket and asking yourself, Is this really worth it? They are won by clawing against opponents on game day and sometimes fighting among teammates at practices. They are won with evolutionary changes: faster and stronger players, better practice facilities, healthier training tables, more understanding of current needs.

Notre Dame will win another football championship someday. But there will never be another Irish team like the championship team in 1988. Many consider that team one of the best ever, and the numbers support it. We defeated teams when they were no. 1, no. 2, and no. 3 in the polls on the way to a 12–0 record.

Three players won consensus all-American honors: defensive end Frank Stams, offensive tackle Andy Heck, and linebacker Michael Stonebreaker. Three others—defensive tackle Chris Zorich, running back Ricky Watters, and linebacker Wes Pritchett—also received national honors that season.

Amazingly, thirty players who played on that team were drafted into the NFL. Most of them went on to distinguished careers, including Watters, Zorich, Stams, Heck, Raghib (Rocket) Ismail, Todd Lyght, Rod Smith, Pat Terrell, Anthony Johnson, and Tim Grunhard. Defensive Coordinator Barry Alvarez became a Hall of Fame head coach at Wisconsin.

Lou Holtz went on to finish with one hundred victories (against only thirty losses) for the Irish and established himself as one of the all-time greats in coaching anywhere. Lou could spot and mold talent. He is a master motivator, which is evident in a 243-127-7 all-time record and also in his popularity as a speaker. It's also evident in how many of the players he coached went on to great jobs and productive lives. He values those results as much as Irish victories.

Most of my Irish teammates went on to successes in their lives after football. Many are millionaires, and many are rich with charitable endeavors. I think of them as career winners. It epitomizes the wonderful spirit of Notre Dame when you see how they have used all their campus experiences to push forward, past football glories, to also become successful professionals and family men.

Thirty members being drafted is an amazing achievement. But it wasn't the biggest. Irish athletes are just as focused on becoming quality individuals in every part of their daily lives. Notre Dame graduates are winners, whether they are athletes or not. The men and women are leaders in their jobs and active in their churches and their communities. They model that the Notre Dame campus is like no other place in the world.

Every player on our championship team had gifts. That includes me. I don't say that boastfully. God granted me great physical gifts. But I took everything seriously. I used God's gifts to the best of my abilities. Thousands of athletes are blessed with physical gifts, but not the motivation to push them toward a championship and a college degree at the same time.

The Irish had the motivation. Our gifts were harnessed and honed through work ethics. We pushed one another, bled together, worked out together, and prayed together.

Players make big sacrifices in going to a great institution. You may not be *the man*; you may have to play a role. Both of the other linebackers that I started with—Michael Stonebreaker and Wes Pritchett—were all-Americans. The other regular linebacker, Cedric Figaro, was a 245-pound monster. I remember we were always serious on the field, always edgy. Linebackers are like that. We all wanted to play every down, yet we all sacrificed our own abilities at times for the betterment of the team.

Sometimes your successes were measured in team victories rather than great personal stats. I made 335 tackles and ten interceptions during my three years of varsity football in high school. My best game in college was 12 tackles versus Pitt in my junior season, when I started eleven games. I was credited with 150 tackles in my career at Notre Dame.

One of the best moments of my career came after Lou assembled the team and asked how hard the players were working out. "I bet you that Flash didn't miss one day of lifting," I remember Lou saying. "He didn't," said the training coach. "He's always here."

A lot of players worked out half-heartedly. They'd come in for twenty minutes and leave. I thought I'd be cheating the team if I didn't go the full ninety minutes, doing the repetitions and lifting every pound that I could.

Some of the players had such natural ability that they thought they could slack off. That was a prevailing attitude in my first two years at Notre Dame. Players of that level should realize there are thousands who never get the opportunity to do so. You have to wonder how much greater some would've been if they had worked harder.

Coming into that final season, I was just eating and lifting and was in the best shape of my life. I weighed about 224 pounds at my top in college (but most times, I played at about 210) and I topped out at 410 pounds in the bench press. That was second on the team only to Zorich. My top weight was built between spring and fall practices, but it was gone as soon as two-a-day practices started. If you can maintain weight and strength, that is fabulous. But I couldn't do it no matter what I ate. I couldn't eat enough steaks or drink enough milkshakes.

I often played as a linebacker and hybrid defensive end when I weighed only about 210. Speed and explosiveness were my best weapons. A newspaper article from my years at Notre Dame said the coaches considered me the strongest player pound for pound on the team. We had to find the time to get our workouts in. Some players did it early in the morning. My class schedule was heavy in the mornings, so that dictated that I lifted weights in the afternoon. That was just before our practices during the spring and fall. I had to do that every day, no matter the season. In prior years, it was obvious that we weakened in the last few games of the season. Coach Holtz did a good job of teaching us ways to enhance our weight and strength.

Here are some of my best memories and observations of my time with the Irish that were crucial and essential in building our championship team:

Athletic Recruiting Is Essential for Success

Every coach has had to battle Notre Dame's position that athletes will be treated no differently than normal students. There was no athletic dorm. We took day classes like everyone else. We were all expected to graduate.

Yet the coaches began to put forth the argument that we needed to change to succeed because the world of college football was changing quickly. The teams we were playing against were getting bigger, stronger, faster, and more talented.

When you are not doing well, administrators tend to listen more. They hear the fans too. Notre Dame had to start taking chances on athletes who could take us further but weren't as academically prepared as in the past.

Build a Cohesive Team

My aggressiveness at practices led to a brawl that had to be stopped by Coach Faust during my first season at Notre Dame. Here's how I remember it. While I was on the scout defense at 188 pounds, I raced around 320-pound starting offensive left tackle Mike Perrino to sack the quarterback. Then I did it again and tackled Pinkett just as he got the ball. I realized something was going to happen as we are running the play for the fourth straight time. I was sweating; it was hot. This time, I decided to go right at Mike.

He came at me 100 percent. We hit head-on and kept going. He pushed me over, and I bounced back up and started wrestling. I got him on his back. Then Mark Bavaro ran up and cleaned my clock, knocking me off Perrino. That was when running backs Chris Smith and Mark Brooks rushed up and hit Bavaro. Then everything turned into a huge brawl.

The defensive line coach came over and immediately asked, "What happened to you out there? Did you know Perrino was a wrestling champion?"

I had no idea, and we laughed about it. Perrino was the biggest player many of us had ever seen. Every young player was in awe of him.

In some ways, the brawl scene was ugly, because it basically turned into a black-versus-white issue. That wouldn't accomplish anything. We needed to be a team. Any racial divisions were like poison.

Perrino and I became great friends. It's almost a rule that you do after situations like that. You respect each other after battling each other. The same went for Bavaro, who went on to become the epitome of a tight end in the NFL.

On the field, he was rugged, tough, and nasty. He didn't talk. I see him today, and he's really mild mannered and cool.

Embracing Diversity

Lou immediately addressed any divisions in our team. He wouldn't allow segregation between black and white players in the dining halls.

Lou would room me with a white linebacker when we stayed in hotels. He would pair up people who were uncomfortable with each other. Those things would force us to have better conversations. The effort was to develop the team rather than just all-star players. All-Americans and third-stringers were best friends. Lou forced us to do more team functions together. That included quiet-time meditations on the night before games.

The defense often visited Coach Alvarez's house. That certainly built unity.

The whole team would come together the night before games to do subliminal relaxation exercises that included ocean and wind sounds.

Lou would calmly speak to us, helping us visualize success the next day. "You're sitting next to Jesus . . . you are going to have a great game," Lou said. "Imagine sacking the quarterback or running so hard through tackles to touchdowns. You can do it."

Preparations the Day before Battle

The day before the game, Coach Holtz instituted another change that I think helped us win the title. He had the team bussed out of town on the Friday night before home games. The reason was, nothing was more important than getting a good night's sleep and getting mentally prepared.

Up to that point, we had been forced to stay in the campus seminary on those nights before games when campus activity would skyrocket. One reason we had to move was that our dorm rooms had our names on the door. My roommate, Reggie Ward, and I would often have to answer the door after well-meaning friends or fans would knock to see if we were in.

We started staying at the Holiday Inn in Plymouth, which was about thirty miles south of the campus. We occupied every room at the hotel. Like Holiday Inn's new slogan, we did get a good night's sleep because there were no distractions.

Lou had total control of the team that way. There was no way to get back and find a teammate at a 3:00 AM party before a game. Nothing was more important than getting a good night's sleep and getting mentally prepared.

Our final practice would be at 3:00 PM on Fridays. The walk-through would be light and loose, with players throwing the ball around and racing one another.

After practice, we'd eat steaks, pasta, and a shrimp dinner on campus, then meet at the practice facility with our overnight bags to be transported to our Holiday. Once we arrived, we'd watch a film like *Patton* or something else to motivate us. Right before retiring for the evening, Lou would lead a twenty-minute mental relaxation session with all players to help us relax and visualize our anxiously anticipated breathtaking performance.

We were always prepared for Game Day.

You Are What You Eat

Coach realized he needed to change the training table and amazed us by making it happen. We used to eat the same food as every other student; we just came in later to the dining hall. (Sometimes hours later!)

The reality was that players burn thousands of calories a day and need far more calories than the average student. Lou asked us what food we wanted and needed to get stronger. We wanted staples such as steaks, waffles, french toast, shrimp, and ribs. When we got to the table after he took over, we were served "all we could eat" of those kinds of foods every day. We were getting more than enough calories, but I am not quite sure a dietician today would agree with our food selection and its sustainability for positive weight gain.

A Leader Must Be a Motivator

Players were always asking Lou to cut practices short in a semiserious way. I remember him telling the team once in the week before our annual game against Michigan, "I called Bo [Schembechler] today, and Bo asked how our practice was going. He said, 'My kids want to skip practice today.' Bo wouldn't allow it. So I told him I am going back and telling my team that I can't let you not practice."

It helps to understand that the Michigan Wolverines rank first all-time in victories, and Notre Dame is third. (Texas is second.) We both have eleven championships. The Irish have the fewest losses of any team. We've been playing since 1887.

Michigan defeated us 24–23 in 1986, Lou's first year at Notre Dame, but we won the next two meetings, 26–7 and 19–17.

The next day at practice, Coach Holtz said, "We called Bo today and told him we aren't practicing. He said that should really help us be relaxed and ready for the game."

Coach Holtz was always using things like that to help us stay motivated and loose.

Communicate and Embrace Your Traditions

Every game we played at Notre Dame was tough. One reason was that many players on other teams had dreamed of playing there, and they were going to prove they should have gotten an offer to go there. We typified the championship student-athlete.

It was unbelievable the respect other institutions gave to Notre Dame. They felt you should be the leader. There was a positive image that permeated throughout the world.

Every time we ran behind Coach Holtz across the field on Game Days and knelt for a quick prayer in the end zone, millions of fans around the world were there with us. That's a real, real exciting moment. That's what you hear about as a recruit.

The greatest players in history have played on the grass at Notre Dame. Knute Rockne gave speeches there. So did Frank Leahy and Dan Devine and Ara Parseghian.

Understand How to Prepare for War

Notre Dame tradition makes players feel like kings. Their gold helmets are painted by students with real flecks of gold. Their pants and jerseys are laid out, along with polished shoes, in the same stalls as legends from the past.

It's tradition that we all attend mass together on campus. It could be a dorm or at the Sacred Heart Basilica. After mass, fans line up from the chapel to the stadium and greet the players. The mass and the walk are so serene. There's a sense of silence, of humbleness, a quiet before the storm. Everyone is edgy on their way as they prepare mentally for performing before a national audience. That includes the coaches, who walk back and forth in the locker room. They are as anxious as we are. They clap hands and slap backs.

Players all react differently as they suit up. Some just sit, holding a rosary while they are thinking and praying. Some players, even big-time stars, vomit regularly before games. Some joke around a bit to cut the tension.

Practice Makes Perfect

It was a necessity to build modern practice fields and weight rooms for the Irish to succeed. Other institutions, such as our archrivals Miami and USC, were getting more cutting-edge facilities and equipment. They had faster athletes. They had the built-in advantage of warm weather throughout the year.

Holtz asked for new practice facilities, including an indoor site, and got it (albeit after I was there). Zorich tells the story that Holtz didn't like to practice indoors very much, even though it impressed recruits. The team would still practice outside even when it was hot, raining, or snowing. "We'd always ask him, 'Let's practice inside because the weather is so bad,'" Zorich said. "He'd say, 'That's for specccccialllll occasions.' There weren't very many special occasions."

Modern facilities are now more important than ever. In this day and age, a recruit makes his selection based on the bling of locker rooms, practice turf vs. grass, and game rooms. It's a major factor.

Find Your Winning Formula

Our followers were spoiled by Coach Holtz. He made his system work for the title team, but he immediately had to start working on the future the minute that we won.

Every coach before current coach Brian Kelly has struggled to find the winning formula in a quickly changing field. Simply put, you have to change when you hit a period of lower productivity. Coach Bob Davie, who followed Holtz, faced that when he coached the Irish from 1997 to 2001.

So did Tyrone Willingham (2002–2004) and Charlie Weis (2005–2009).

The Irish were falling behind. Every four or five years or so, a new coach came on, and a big change was needed.

The kids today take harder looks at facilities, at records in the last few years, and at whether a team can compete from year to year. They want to see Jumbotrons. They ask themselves, Why would I go to Notre Dame and not these other places?

The program under Kelly has become more flexible in many ways. But he is demanding and successful. He matched Holtz by making it to the title game in his third season.

Without Respect, You Got NOTHING!

No showboating. That was an ironclad rule at Notre Dame. Whenever we scored, an Irish player just handed the ball to a referee. It was no big deal. There was no dancing because we had seen this before. It's simply what was expected.

It was also a matter of respecting our opponents. We showed that in another traditional way. Win or lose, after every home game, the Irish raise their helmets and salute fans in the stands as the band plays "Notre Dame, Our Mother."

Kelly Did It His Way

You have to see success, believe in it, in order to truly experience it.

"A leader has to have a vision and plan to get there," Lou Holtz said about taking over at Notre Dame. "I had a vision where I wanted to take the program." Three years later, that vision became a reality with a national championship. It was the eleventh for the Irish.

Kelly has a vision to resurrect a program that had gone through five fairly mediocre seasons. It was amazing to watch the team progress toward a bowl game in his first season. The Irish appeared to be headed to more mediocrity—at 1–3 and 4–5, with some frustrating losses late in games—before winning three straight regular-season games, including defeating USC for the first time in twelve seasons.

It's noteworthy that the hot streak in 2010 started after the Irish's only week off during the season. That preparation time obviously made a major difference.

Notre Dame defeated the no. 15 Utes, 28–3.

The Irish then defeated Army and USC before walloping our old nemesis, Miami, at 33–17 in the Sun Bowl to finish at 8–5.

The defense allowed nearly four hundred yards per game in starting at 4–5 but held opposing offenses to about half that in the perfect 4–0 finish.

It can't be oversold how much that successful finish meant to the program. It was so important to get to a bowl game because the team would have nearly three more weeks of practice time.

Kelly said the players didn't need to be pushed. They were ready to practice each day with the result being a final statement victory. That kind of finish builds confidence and establishes a winning identity. Those are all positive signs of good coaching.

Ironically, Kelly inherited a situation similar to Holtz taking over after five so-so seasons under Gerry Faust. Kelly's vision focuses on fundamentals, close-knit teamwork, and effective practices. Just like Holtz did, Kelly started off with predawn practices. Players and fans can tell exactly the way they feel by body language on the sidelines. Those coaches won't accept mediocrity.

Kelly is doing it his way. He had great success before in building programs at University of Cincinnati, Central Michigan, and Grand Valley State. His record at those three institutions was 171-57-2.

He led Grand Valley State to national championships in 2002 and 2003 in NCAA Division II, compiling a 28–1 record along the way. He led Cincinnati to a 12–0 regular-season record and Big East title in 2009 after beginning the season unranked.

CHAPTER 9

Title Game, Hula Bowl

THIS WAS IT—OUR heavyweight title fight. We had reached the national championship game. And the atmosphere was unlike anything I'd ever experienced.

The glamour and glitz, the lights and cameras, the inquiring reporters and adoring fans—all were omnipresent for the days leading up to the Sunkist Fiesta Bowl at Tempe, Arizona. Both teams were undefeated: Notre Dame was 11–0, and West Virginia was also 11–0. We were ranked no. 1, with a team that kept growing more confident every week.

The Mountaineers were ranked no. 3 and featured an offense that had steamrolled other teams all season. It reminded me in many ways of going to those fights in Atlantic City and watching my brother Victor when I was a young teenager: two great athletes ready to bring everything into the ring.

I close my eyes and picture bright lights, vibrant colors, heat and haze, screaming fans waiting for a knockout. I remember the gold pants and blue jerseys and similarly colored balloons reaching toward the sky during the pregame ceremony. My dad and younger brother, Chris, shared in the joy of that championship game with me. It was so special. We all had been together to see Victor fight. We were together now. This time, it was my stage. I was in the championship ring.

The weekly spectacle was something the Irish players became used to at Notre Dame. Every home game at Notre Dame was filled with energy and glamour. And it was always exciting to enter an opponent's stadium too. That was especially so at places like Michigan, where there were more than one hundred thousand people pulling for us to lose. You can certainly feed off both energies. But this neutral-site game was different. Every move was amplified in the time we spent there in preparation for the game.

It was a blur of activity. You couldn't turn around without being asked a question by a reporter, it seemed, or being approached by a proud Irish fan. There were practices, dinners, signings, and banquets with West Virginia players. Almost every minute was scripted, planned out. Get on the bus, get off the bus. I was so excited that it was hard to sleep.

Some of us players did find a way to sneak away and get into a late-night issue that could have had drastic consequences. But more about that later.

It was hot in Arizona, especially after practicing for several weeks in wintry South Bend. But we hardly knew the difference. It's almost like we were walking on air. You could call it an air of confidence. West Virginia had no chance in our minds.

We were so prepared, so confident, and so talented that we knew that we'd bring home Notre Dame's eleventh championship and its first in eleven seasons. Our fans were everywhere, offering encouraging words. Dad and Chris made many new friends. It's just my estimate, but I bet the Mountaineers' fans were outnumbered by at least 3–1. We had the home-field energy going. We were defending our turf.

Our confidence was booming. We already knocked off no. 1 Miami, 31–30, in a game considered one of the best in college history.

The Hurricanes had entered Notre Dame Stadium with a thirty-five-game winning streak in regular-season games. We finished the regular season by triumphing 27–10 over no. 2 USC. That last victory came over a Trojans team that was ranked no. 2 but was favored by oddsmakers to beat us.

We had won quite handily before ninety-four thousand fans on their turf, the Los Angeles Coliseum, with two of our stars (Ricky Watters and Tony Brooks) benched for disciplinarian reasons, as I already mentioned. We had jelled as a team in that game like no other time I can remember in my seasons with the Irish.

We had one major reason to be optimistic. To beat the Trojans, our defense had to slow down quarterback Rodney Peete, a fleet-footed scrambler who also had a strong passing arm. We now would face West Virginia quarterback Major Harris, who featured many of the same winning traits.

All we had to do to stop him was keep doing what we were doing. We had just stopped Peete. Now we could stop Harris. There was another reason for such optimism on defense: our own starting quarterback, Tony Rice, mirrored Peete and Harris in his ability to run an option offense. That meant we saw him play every day—in practice, in scrimmages, in spring games, during real games, and on film.

The defense already had the map in their minds how to stop that kind of talent. We had two all-Americans at linebacker (Michael Stonebreaker and Wes Pritchett) and also two on the defensive line (Frank Stams and Chris Zorich).

West Virginia certainly had rolled to an amazing season behind a killer offense that averaged 43 points. It scored 62 in its season opener. The Mountaineers also had scored 59, 55, and 51 (twice) in winning other games.

They had defeated Penn State 51–30 to rise to 8–0. That victory was considered the biggest ever for West Virginia football. Yet the Nittany Lions weren't ranked, and West Virginia had defeated only one top 20 team all season long. This was a case where our stronger schedule certainly made a difference. The way I saw it, the only possible way that West Virginia could win was to run over our defense or pull away several turnovers. Those things weren't going to happen. We simply wouldn't allow them to wrestle the title trophy and the memories away from us. History proves that we didn't.

Our defense frustrated the Mountaineers' offense for most of the game, and our offense was effective as we triumphed in the title game on January 2, 1989. The score was 34–21. Our defense forced seven punts and gave up 200 yards less than West Virginia's average of 482 coming into the game. Rice did a lot of damage with his running, his arm, and his leadership. Stams had a big day on defense, and they both were MVPs.

It was muggy and kind of hot as we played in the late afternoon. I was too pumped up to even notice. We ate quiche the night before and attended Mass together in the early afternoon. After the game, I found out that it was so miserable in the stands that Dad and Chris had to move.

Much of what I recall now came from watching television replays at my dad's house. It makes me proud every time I hear the announcer talk about the stellar play on defense of Frank Stams and Flash Gordon.

I remember running out onto the field with the team for the final time and my name being announced. I remember Coach Lou Holtz was clapping and running around as he cheered us up. He kept it up the whole game. I was filled with such gratitude to be on the field at the start. That season had its ups and downs, but I was there at the end. The picture is still fresh on my mind when Defensive Coordinator Barry Alvarez told me, "Darrell, I am going to start you." I was back in starting position for the biggest game of my career. That said everything for the hard work I'd put in.

Sometimes, the season had been exhilarating, and sometimes it had been humiliating. But I didn't quit or moan. That's so often what people do. I learned more than anything that I never quit. When I came out on the field for the title game, I felt a sense of gratitude and adulation.

The linebacking crew at Notre Dame was built on sacrifice. You may not be "the man, the starter," but you may have to play a role. We all had to sacrifice our own abilities for the betterment of the team.

The first play was a pitchout, and it became me against Major Harris, one on one. I made the tackle and remember it was such a great feeling to be back starting. What a confidence builder. I felt fast, and every defender on the Irish was spot on their game.

Harris was their big star, and I had already found out that I could get to him. Fortunately, I tackled him for a sack later at a critical point in the second half. By then, Harris was really hurting. Stonebreaker had smashed him into the ground and separated his left shoulder on

West Virginia's third play from scrimmage. That certainly had to affect his performance. That script was similar to the USC rout. Frank Stams leveled Peete so hard after an early interception that the USC quarterback never played up to his ability the rest of the game. Those clean plays really proved that we were invincible. Our defense was simply too good.

A field goal by Billy Hackett and a touchdown run by Anthony Johnson gave us a 9–0 lead in the first quarter. Rodney Culver extended the lead with a five-yard run. Charlie Bauman made it 16–3 with a field goal for West Virginia. We soon countered as Tony Rice hit Raghib Ismail on a twenty-nine-yard touchdown pass.

Rice connected on several long passes in the game—something that surprised West Virginia. A last-second field goal by Bauman made the score 23–6 at halftime, and we were on our way. It was electric as we jogged off the field.

There were smiles and back slaps, yet we were surprisingly subdued in the locker room. We were focused as Lou made a short speech. He really didn't need to say much. We had done our jobs well, but we knew that overconfidence could hurt us.

One problem with major games like that is that the halftime is longer. There are also long delays for advertisements between possessions. You can cool off too much and give up momentum if you don't watch out.

Our defense had been filled with question marks coming into the season, but we now had gone six quarters of shutting down a gifted quarterback. Despite Harris's injury, we expected a rally. It was inevitable against an undefeated team that had some stellar players. Reggie Ho hit a field goal in the third quarter.

A critical juncture in the game came after the Mountaineers had closed to 26–13 and soon made an interception in our territory. It was our only turnover of the game, and it could have spelled disaster. West Virginia had its strongest momentum of the game and could have turned the game around with a touchdown.

On the first play, I pushed off a defender and wrapped up Harris for a two-yard loss as he ran an option play. It was considered a sack because Harris still could have passed.

On the next play, he threw a pass into the end zone that was deflected by Stan Smagala. Then Stams and Arnold Ale sacked Harris for a twelve-yard loss. That took the Mountaineers out of field goal range and effectively ended West Virginia's chances.

West Virginia coach Don Nehlen told reporters afterward that the two-sack series was a major turning point. "Had we put something on the board there, we're in business," he explained. "That was a monster."

Rice finished the Irish scoring and gave us a 34–13 lead in the fourth quarter by making a jump pass for three yards to Frank Jacobs for a touchdown and then running in a two-point conversion. Harris was on the bench when West Virginia scored again.

The celebration on the field was a blur too. I was carried off by Dave Jandrick and Mickey Anderson, I believe. It felt great. It was so great to win.

The championship victory all came together as scripted, as we had confidently foreseen it. We started the season expecting to go undefeated (as you always do). Realistically, there were only two possible games we could have lost.

As often happens, we could have easily lost in the opener at home to no. 9, Michigan. Ho made a forty-nine-yard field goal with a little more than a minute left. The Wolverines came right back, though. Their kicker sailed a forty-eight-yard field goal effort just wide of the upright on the final play. We could still have made the championship with that loss, I believe, but the season wouldn't have been as magical.

Truth to tell, the month leading up to the championship game was the most fun of any time I had at Notre Dame. The practices were the loosest. School was out much of the time, so the team practically had the run of campus. Coach Holtz's game plan included keeping us relaxed and fresh. He's a humorous guy, but he was cracking more jokes and smiling than ever before with that game.

This master motivator constantly told us in his words and actions, "We will win this game. We will be the national champion." He even had us spend time practicing how we'd be carried off the field after our victory. Pick a senior, he told the underclassmen, on a chilly afternoon in South Bend. "We want them on your shoulders." Yes, it was orchestrated.

It was a change in character for Coach Holtz. Traditionally, he would take on his famed aw-shucks demeanor all week: "I don't know if we can beat them." This time, he did that with the newspapers and television reporters, but not with us.

He kept repeating that this team shouldn't even be in the game with us. We are way too focused and organized, he said. Our abilities to execute were higher. Our athletes were better, and we were more disciplined. It was the first time in the three years leading up to this game that we saw him so relaxed.

It would be wrong, though, to say we were overconfident. We simply knew that we were the better team. We were more disciplined. We had thirty players who would be drafted in the NFL, including two first rounders and eight second rounders.

It could have been a huge mistake to run hard practices for the month leading up to the title game. We could have gotten overprepared, gotten tight. We had the momentum, so we rode it. That's strong, and it's subtle. Actually, the victory was easier than any of us could have predicted. But looking back, we were destined to do something great.

The new attitude started immediately after we had defeated USC. Coach told us to take a little time off. We stayed in California for a while. He allowed us to go home for a few days to celebrate the holidays with our families. He deftly prepared us in every way to win our championship.

Coach was a master at motivating his teams to win after facing major adversity. There was no better example of that than how we pulled together at the aforementioned USC game.

The next step after winning the title, I thought, would be a shot at playing in the NFL. Little did I know that celebratory night in Arizona, but my football career would come to an end less than a week later and another world away.

This is how that happened.

I had just gotten back home to New Jersey two days later when I got a call from Coach Holtz's secretary. He wanted to know if I could get to Hawaii because a linebacker hadn't shown up for practices in the Hula Bowl all-star game.

She said that if I could catch a flight in two hours, I was invited to play. Of course, I would have rowed a boat to Hawaii to accept the unexpected honor. I didn't even have enough clean clothes, but I made that flight.

It was hard to believe on the flight there. One day I was winning a national championship, and then I was asked to play in a game that featured players such as NFL Hall of Famers Deion Sanders and Troy Aikman.

I practiced and played next to some of the best players in the world—guys who went on to fifteen-year careers and made millions of dollars in the pros. There were big chunky linemen with biceps and necks like they were pros already. There were guys with unbelievable talent levels all in the same place. I knew I belonged at that level because Lou had brought in top-notch, high-level coaches. Their next step was the big time.

We were so fortunate to have Alvarez as defensive coordinator that title season. He was one of the best coaches at Xs and Os, one of the best preparers of any coach for a game. It's certainly appropriate that Holtz and Alvarez were inducted into the College Football Hall of Fame in back-to-back seasons.

Alvarez allowed Holtz to concentrate on the offense. He was one of the only position coaches who motivated me. He got me to play at a high level consistently. He told me, "You're going to make a lot of money if you can keep playing at this level."

I thought, *Man, I am on my way.* I had no reason to think otherwise as I was on my way during the heady flight to Hawaii.

My college football world changed quickly. I found out the strict NCAA rules didn't relate to me as soon as I landed in Honolulu.

A man picked me up at the airport, who was adorned with Notre Dame attire. He was very friendly and praised my play in helping lead the Irish to the title. "I am so glad you could make it. You deserve to be here," he said. That felt great to hear.

He took me straight to a store where he insisted on buying me two suits and other clothes. There would be banquets to attend and hundreds of people to meet that week and in the near future, the man said. I was on my way to another level.

This pregame scene was very different. Instead of Notre Dame fans, there were professional scouts and agents everywhere. I had concerns about taking the free clothes, but it was immediately confirmed that his actions were within NCAA guidelines after finishing my career with Notre Dame. The season was over. Everything was legal.

I was certain that I could play in the NFL. This was a step toward that.

It was obvious that Sanders was the cream of the crop. He was simply the best all-around athlete I'd ever seen. He knew he was going to become a star athlete and personality, and he wasn't afraid to display his confidence. He wasn't afraid of anything, period. He was an untouchable. "Don't worry about me!" I remember him yelling out about getting hit during the game.

He had already attracted some great attention. He waved cash around on the bus ride before the Hula Bowl. I heard a story about him soon after the game that I can easily believe. He reportedly arrived for a combine test in a limousine. He walked in, stretched a little, and ran 4.29 in the 40-yard dash. Then he left.

The practices were fun, and I was looking forward to the Hula Bowl. The scouts talked positively about me as a linebacker in the NFL, and a couple of big hits (administered by me) in the game could propel me toward a higher draft position.

But I never got that chance. The sun was hot, and I remember that sweat was rolling off my brow. There was little hoopla unlike the title game. The stands weren't full. That's something I wasn't used to. Every game sold out at Notre Dame.

There was a lot more pushing and shoving on tackles than I was used to. That's how I hyperextended my right knee while trying to make a tackle. That one event effectively ended my football career.

It happened in one of those pileups that you see a lot with seven defensive guys and five offensive guys pushing until someone goes to the ground. I made a solid hit, but I didn't put the runner down. More and more players began to surround him, and I got caught up in that group. I always wore knee braces to protect them, but that proved to be a detriment in this case.

This time, my foot got caught in the turf. The weight of everyone pushing and pushing was coming my way, but I couldn't pull my leg out. Then the whole crowd fell on it.

I knew something was hurt, but I tried to still play through it. The amazing thing is, you're not supposed to get hurt in an all-star game. After that, it got worse and worse. I talked to the trainer about the pain in my knee later in the game.

I didn't need to have surgery, but I needed to rehabilitate it. My life's focus changed in the moment of that injury and the days that followed. I knew that I couldn't attend any combines or try out for NFL teams, but I kept it low-key for a while. The whole experience was a shock and an eye-opener about my future.

I really began to reflect on my career—my academic career. Notre Dame made more sense in my life. Maybe there was a reason why I put forth such effort that had nothing to do with the pros. The lesson was preparation for life after athletics. It served to give me a richer life.

So many other athletes at the all-star game weren't even going to graduate. I was way ahead because I left Notre Dame later that summer of 1989 with two degrees—a BS in economics and business that I had earned in 1988 and a graduate diploma in science of administration that I received in August of 1989.

I wanted to start my professional life. Even after my knee was rehabilitated, I didn't even attempt to try out for the NFL, and I've never regretted it. Instead, I started on the path toward becoming a hard-charging lawyer and child-focused CEO rather than a hard-hitting linebacker.

It taught me again that you never know what change can await you.

CHAPTER 10

Learn When to Move On

MY FATHER'S WORDS stung like freezing rain. "You don't belong here anymore. It's time for you to leave." Say what? You certainly don't expect a loved one to put it on the line so bluntly. But my dad did. And I am forever grateful that he did. He said those words as we sat in a car outside the shop that had supported our family for so many years.

I hadn't planned on moving back home to New Jersey after college. I had planned on working out for NFL teams and getting drafted. I was convinced that I had the strength, speed, and smarts to make a lot of money with my football talents.

The reality is, I wasn't prepared to hit the job market in the summer of 1989 after earning my graduate degree in business. The job market wasn't strong for anyone at that time. So I returned to eastern New Jersey with the thoughts of helping my dad run his burgeoning automotive business. Soon I was getting into a comfort zone. My dream job on Wall Street could wait.

It was fun to reconnect with old friends and revel in the glow—and social attention—of being a national champion football player. Life was pretty easy: I had a free place to live in a spacious home with my father.

I was too self-centered to notice my dad's angst. I'm sure his friends and customers were asking, "Hey, Gordon, what's your kid going to do with his life? Didn't he get a big degree from a great university?"

Dad and I had just come back from lunch when he turned and said his piece, which essentially was that I shouldn't be working at a garage when I had a master's degree from one of the best universities in the world. No matter how nicely it's delivered in situations like that, all you can hear is, "Get out."

It makes you mad. It hurts. But it is often exactly what you need to hear.

Sometimes it takes tough talk, a kick in the butt, to make you move on and move forward with your life. I used the hurt as a motivation, just as when Lou Holtz informed me that he didn't want me coming back for my senior season, and just as when the Notre Dame representative said I didn't have the academic background (yet) that it would take to succeed there. Each of those times, I was able to make the changes needed to earn what I desired. Each time you persevere after something negative happens, you grow more confident for making future changes and for conquering other mountains.

Dad's request for me to leave proved to be major stimuli for change in my life. Without that shove, who knows where I'd be? It certainly wouldn't be where I am today. I realize now that the job of a parent is to deliver bad news as well as hugs and high-fives. It may be many years, even decades, before your children understand it.

I was drawn back to my home area because it was safe. My mom and other relatives loved that. I moved into the house my dad shared with his partner, Diane, because my mom had sold our childhood duplex and moved into a one-bedroom apartment.

It was easy living in one way, but also taxing on me psychologically. I was still working through my feelings about the situation following my parents' breakup a decade before. I was self-centered and immature. I remember several times forgetting to pass on messages to my dad from Diane when she called the shop.

The summer before, I'd stayed with them and left phone bills from calling Notre Dame friends from California and Texas and Ohio and Hawaii. There weren't cell phones with free minutes at night and on weekends then. There was no email or Facebook to connect constantly and cheaply. Phone calls were expensive.

In no uncertain terms, my dad demanded that I pay him back the $140 or so in phone bills from that last summer before the championship season. It was tough coming up with that amount. Athletes at top universities such as Notre Dame seldom have cash, and there are few chances to earn it during the school year. That fact has been publicized of late as the NCAA considers ways to give players a financial hand.

My dad was trying to teach me how to be responsible and not take advantage of others. It certainly wasn't responsible or remotely considerate for me to leave him phone bills. But I didn't see it that way then.

With many things in life, you have to live through the tough situations to understand them and to learn to make positive changes. That's called maturity.

My dad wanted me to achieve something higher—something that I couldn't find by living near my hometown again. That's when he delivered the message for me to leave and discover my own path to success. That was a major turning point in my life.

It's common for people who achieve great success to realize they must break away from home and find it on their own.

I was forced to quickly formulate a plan of action that could carry me toward a career befitting my education. I called on Frank Eck, the CEO of Advanced Drainage Systems, whom I had befriended while attending Notre Dame. I had met him through networking at the tailgate parties that surround Notre Dame home football games. Our relationship had quickly become close. He immediately said, "I'll fly you out." I interviewed with his executive staff at the headquarters near Columbus, Ohio, and soon was working my first full-time job as their corporate safety director for facilities throughout the United States. Frank steered Advanced Drainage to great successes as its leader. It now does more than $1 billion in sales per year.

Unbeknownst to me at the time, my father had discreetly called Frank and asked him to watch out for me without coddling me. I really didn't find out about it until one of my daily chats with Dad as I make the hour-long drive to work. My dad told Frank that he didn't want me to experience an unrealistic work life of jets, big homes, and great money. He asked Frank to help his twenty-two-year-old son understand the value of hard work and what was necessary to achieve true successes in our complex world.

My dad's reasoning was that my life at Notre Dame had been a dream athletic trip that rarely required any giving from my end other than autographs. My dad's request was so appropriate because Frank had taken such a fatherly role with me during my career. Eck was known for being a mentor to many players, including Chris Zorich and others, and a huge benefactor to his university. "He would do whatever he could to help the athletes," said his son, Frank Eck Jr., a dear friend who serves on the board of Wernle Youth & Family Treatment Center. "He'd help recruit within bounds of the school and NCAA. He was always big in athletics—baseball and tennis too."

He was also big in other charitable ways for Notre Dame. Many buildings on the campus carry on the name of my great mentor, who died in 2007. He embodied so much and taught me so much about having good character, about listening, about sacrificing. It's been shown through studies that those personal characteristics are the most necessary for making changes that succeed long-term.

I'll never forget how I met Frank.

Rather than partying after games, I was more into networking. I used to go around to some of the parking lot get-togethers. I met Frank by talking with alumni after a game one early evening. We just connected. He was so open, and I came to learn so much from him about being a leader and a forward-thinking person.

I was always in a hurry to get places. Frank gave me a sense of calm about my life pursuits. He'd often remind me that he didn't become chief executive officer of Advanced Drainage until his fifties. He exposed me to greatness and being a leader. He taught me about being a caring, ethical, and critical-thinking CEO with a sharp pencil.

One of the skills that I learned from him was the immense value of planning—of seeing the future of your business. He had yearly strategic planning sessions. We now do, too, at Wernle. I plan my yearly goals too. Every December, I sit down and ask myself what I want my family and I to accomplish for the next year while living the life that we can afford. I put those written goals under a glass top at home so I can see them. I put a dollar figure to it. The goals have to be reasonable so they can be accomplished.

I have done the same thing in helping two of my nephews reach their goals. My nephews and I strategically work on the question "How can I get where I want to be?" Regardless of the length of time it takes, that age will come. It could be next year, or it could be in five years.

We even have a strategic plan for our family reunion, for our Catalyst for Change event, and for our yearly Wernle tailgate party before the home opener for Notre Dame football. I am honored to help carry on Frank's tailgate tradition of meeting and greeting people.

Traditional events are important for families. We are a reflection of our history. I learned from watching Frank at his tailgaters. Over decades, the events became a normal part of what he did and what his family and friends did.

Wernle has gained some great friends through its tailgaters. We spend $1,000 or so to put them on each September, but the dividends have paid back 1,000 to 1 with the friendships we have gained. We share with benefactors like the Hawk, Sharpe, Eck, and Maley families.

We never know who will show up at our tailgate events. It's so great to reconnect with friends, and it's awesome to meet new people. You never know how people can help each other grow until you meet them and get to understand them. The events bring people together for common cause.

Frank Eck was a shining example. By watching great leaders work, you become a better leader. We often chatted about the parallels we shared in life. We are both natives of New Jersey. He participated in track in the early 1940s and earned a degree in chemical engineering in 1944.

Frank and I shared other similarities besides being student-athletes at Notre Dame and eventually becoming CEOs. Frank got his MBA from Harvard University, and I also did studies there. That's where I received my certification for strategic planning in nonprofit management.

I have learned to be philanthropic like Frank. That changes you. There were so many personal ways he helped people, from Irish players to the secretaries and janitors at his business.

I wanted to give back to society too. It's worthy to go to a nonprofit that you believe in and be a catalyst. I have been on the receiving end for so long in a financial and spiritual sense.

So many of the benefactors for Wernle have given and received too. The Eck tradition carries on with Frank Jr., serving as a valuable member on the Wernle board of directors. He was a great friend in college. For more than twenty years, we've been like family.

My goal to become a CEO really kicked in while spending time with Frank as he showed me around the high-profile business world. He would invite me to fly on a private jet as he traveled around the country while managing his business. It gets contagious when you watch a true entrepreneurial pioneer at work. Frank was instrumental in leading me to think big like a CEO.

I worked four years for him in quality assurance operations and sales. The company transferred me to Cincinnati, Ohio. I ran Advanced Drainage's distribution facility in New Miami, then became a sales representative. "He took an exceptional interest in you," Frank Eck Jr. said. "Your character shines through, and you're a go-getter. That impressed my father."

I soon took another major step in my life: I chose to pursue a law degree and applied to several colleges. I knew that I needed that degree to move my career forward. Frank was thrilled for me. He believed, like other mentors, in following dreams and in being passionate about what you do. Watching him had given me the ability to create a plan to be a CEO one day. Becoming a lawyer was an integral part of that plan.

Frank always said that there was a lot more to management than making profits. He modeled that in so many ways. He always talked about being positive, treating everyone with respect no matter his or her place in life. He never wanted anyone to fail. At the same time, he wanted his company to be the best, so he demanded the best.

"My father was constructive rather than negative," Frank Jr. said. "He'd say, 'Let's look at this problem and see how we can make it better.' He'll work with you. People are successful when they do that rather than being a taskmaster. You can accomplish a lot more by taking an active interest and wanting them to succeed."

Frank Eck's mentoring never stopped. I remember, like yesterday, talking with him one-to-one about my role at Wernle at a restaurant one night. I had wanted to share thoughts with him about my career, to make sure I was going in the right direction. I am impatient about making major achievements, so I was a bit down and disappointed as my progress wasn't as swift as I hoped at Wernle.

I wasn't where I should be, I told him. "I want to be doing some of the things you are. I want to be able to give to others as significantly as you," I clearly recall saying to Frank.

He kind of chuckled, but he definitely took me seriously. He reminded me that he was a lot older than I was when he took over Advanced Drainage and that he wasn't able to seriously give back to Notre Dame until far after that.

"When I took over this facility, I was fifty-five. I wasn't thirty-nine or forty," Frank said. "You are beating yourself up. There's nowhere you need to be yet. One thing I can tell you is that you are probably exactly where you need to be. You are way ahead of me. You have a strong drive. That drive sometimes helps you. Sometimes it doesn't."

Those profound comments really made me see things in a different light and helped me settle down in my life. They made me realize that I needed to continue preparing for success yet also loosen up at the same time. Frank, my dad, and my brother Chris all have taught me to slow down and to enjoy things and let success come to me.

Wanting others to succeed is part of the plan too. Once you've tasted the success, it's time to pass it on. One thing that I can certainly pass on is that success isn't measured in money. That will naturally come when you are a leader in your field. Being a leader also means constantly learning about yourself and reevaluating your goals.

One of my ultimate goals for attending law school was to become a sports agent. But I came to learn through an internship with IMG that I couldn't do that because I believed that to succeed, I'd have to manipulate young people. I wanted to help them, not use them to help me earn money.

The same process of critical thinking made me realize that Wall Street wouldn't work for me either. While learning business acumen from my dad, I had dreamed for a long time of working there. But after earning my bachelor's degree and awaiting my final season of football, I worked for the summer as an intern at the New York Stock Exchange. Coincidentally, that was about the time the movie *Wall Street* had become a megahit, with its focus on greed.

I enjoyed the experience on Wall Street—the three-piece suits and limousine rides to lunch—and know I could have succeeded there. But it wasn't right for me. I don't need private gold-plated bathrooms or mind-blowing expense accounts. I simply don't envy those who've made millions on Wall Street. But I have had some folks who work there tell me they wish they had done more to help people like I have with young people at Wernle.

I haven't made millions of dollars, but I don't care. My family is comfortable. Watching people change is what's priceless to me. It's worth a lot more than money to be a model of good character and to help heal abused and neglected children, to educate them, and to give them hope.

Frank Eck is one of the people who made me realize what's really important in life. I was honored to be a pallbearer at his funeral after he died in 2007, at age eighty-four. Hundreds who were affiliated with Notre Dame, including the university president, attended to honor this great man who was truly one of a kind.

FRANK ECK '44

CHAPTER 11

Law School Impacts

IT'S ALWAYS GREAT to be content and comfortable in your life. Sometimes, though, that is a prescription for mediocrity. A lot of really good football teams finish around .500. Or worse. Often, you need more. You need a kick in the tail to take your life to the next level.

Let me share a great recent example from the NFL. The San Francisco 49ers were a mediocre 6–10 in the 2010 regular season. But with using much the same players, they rose to within a field goal of winning the Super Bowl. They finished with a 14–4 record. It was obvious there was one major difference: they had acquired an amazing motivational and kick-butt coach in Jim Harbaugh. He and his staff pushed the 49ers' game to a higher level.

Often, we need to reassess our lives and decide to kick it to a higher level. It would be great if we could hire a personal coach with a last name like Harbaugh or Holtz. But that's not going to happen. What can happen, though, is motivating yourself and surrounding yourself with positive, supportive people.

Start by questioning yourself, Are you really where you want to be?

That question stuck in my mind like honey on cornbread as I contemplated my future seven years after earning my graduate degree from Notre Dame. I was comfortable, but not content, in my career after college. I'd made steady advances with Advanced Drainage Systems. But I was ready for another challenge. I wasn't satisfied.

To reach successes in your life, it's essential to challenge yourself and to be challenged. I asked myself the following questions:

How badly do you want—or need—to change?

Do you need a change now? Next year? Five years from now?

How would a drastic change impact you and those around you?

That last question was extremely important. It might not be a shrewd move to leave a good job in an iffy economy when you have a wife and three young children to feed. But I wasn't married as I approached my thirtieth birthday, so that didn't figure into the do-it or don't-do-it equation.

When I chose to attend law school, though, I left a great job and was forced to cut down on opportunities to care for my mother. Those were painful decisions that were made with great support from the people I would affect by making a change.

One of the hardest things about change is that many people want the world to change around them. That isn't happening. Famous Russian author Leo Tolstoy was quoted as saying, "Everyone thinks of changing the world, but no one thinks of changing himself or herself."

There's no doubt that some changes come only with personal pain. That certainly was the case when I had to leave my comfort zone as a manager for Advanced Drainage Systems.

The decision to attend law school meant I had to leave a company whose employees had treated me like family. I was well respected and compensated. (Well, maybe not *that* well compensated. It was a first job, of course.) And many people stayed at the company for life. In fact, many of my old colleagues were still there as recently as a few years ago, including my assistant and Frank Eck's executive assistant. I still love stopping by for some hugs and jokes from time to time. It feels good, like taking a walk across a campus on a sunny, warm football day in the fall. Those two taught me things that aren't in any employee handbook, including how to treat women.

As an athlete, you are often surrounded by beautiful women who are vying for your attention and affection. You don't have a lot of spare time for dating. That makes you selfish. You don't learn about romance and about being a giver, as well as a receiver. My surrogate sisters at Advanced Drainage showed me how to give roses and show I cared. Sometimes, I'd buy a dozen roses and give one to each woman in the office. They taught me a lot about being a better man and a better manager.

It wasn't easy to leave. But the simple fact was, we were selling pipe and fabrics. The product wasn't very sexy, compared to my dreams of being a sports agent or Wall Street broker.

I had loftier leadership goals. I wanted to eventually run my own business. I figured a great step in that process would be to go to law school. Like everything, I aimed for the top by applying to Harvard and several other major institutions. There wasn't an immediate slot at Harvard, and I didn't want to wait on late-admission possibilities. So I chose to accept an offer from Northern Kentucky University's Chase School of Law. It allowed me to stay close to Cincinnati.

Frank was the first person I told after being accepted to law school. We had talked about a week before, and I had mentioned I wasn't really satisfied with the direction I was headed. I felt like I could do more and accomplish more in my life, and I told him that I needed to do more work to make a profound effect on society. He asked me to come up for dinner in Columbus.

During that dinner, I told him I was really interested in going to law school and would love to hear his thoughts. He said, "You gotta go. You've got to do it." He was so supportive.

That was a real profound transformation in my life.

Another life transformation would rock my world about the same time.

It was a time in my life I had to make critical decisions.

My mom had nearly died from a heart ailment at home in New Jersey, so I had brought her to live with me in Cincinnati so I could look after her. Despite her infirmities, my mom mirrored Frank's message to me, even though it meant she'd be alone more in Cincinnati: "You gotta go." It was the natural, God-inspired process, she said, just like when she and Dad moved from South Carolina to find a better life.

I knew she needed me, but she knew I needed to keep challenging myself and moving forward in life. She was as adamant that I go as she was when I got the offer to attend Notre Dame a decade before.

She was so thrilled when I left for law school, and her tears were of joy, not of loss. In retrospect, I suspect she sensed that she was being called home soon by God. I bought her a puppy for companionship and asked a friend to check in on her when I couldn't. I'd visit when I could, but law school was amazingly intense.

She died of a heart attack only months after I started to attend Chase.

The days and weeks after her death were extremely challenging. It was a time where I could have taken time away from school, and maybe never gone back. I quickly realized that it was imperative that I get back to school, that I not falter in my dream, that I honor my mom's dream for me. She was a hero. She helped shape me into a proactive person—one who believed that you must make things happen.

She pushed her children to pursue their dreams. She knew full well that often entails changing your environment. That was necessary for me at first, and then for my younger brother, Chris.

The first major step in our life transformation was going away to college—I to Notre Dame and he to Brown University. We had to leave the cocoon—the comfort zone—that we understood at home in New Jersey. I could have stayed near my mom's loving embrace forever near Hillside. It would have been easy.

The moves, though, proved to be outstanding successes for us.

An amazing thing happens after you make profound changes and work hard to succeed. You gain confidence and become a new person. It makes you look for new challenges.

My mom knew all about breaking out of the cocoon. She was tremendously loyal to her home, her family, and her church, so it wasn't easy for her to move to Cincinnati. But she did it because she needed my help.

We didn't have enough time together there, but at least we had eight months. We had some great times, and I am so glad we could share them in her last year. I would have missed so much without her close to me at that time in my life.

When I got back from my mom's funeral, Dean Short, Professor Caryl Yzenbaard, and several other special university workers were open in showing their support for me. That was so important because I was really being challenged with my ability to focus.

I was feeling lonely, in mourning, but that didn't matter. Law school is all about focus and about being attentive to details.

The instructors wanted me to succeed, but they didn't coddle me. That's important, I strongly believe, because success is best when it's earned, not when it's bestowed upon you.

I didn't want any courtesy grades. I needed to prove to myself that I could do the work it took to become a lawyer. It was actions more than words from folks at Chase that helped me through that difficult, soul-searching time.

Professor Yzenbaard was the toughest and most inspiring teacher I've ever dealt with. She had a passion and zeal that made you want to learn everything about her area of expertise, which was property law. That is a fairly boring subject, but she made it exciting. She made me do things I didn't know I could do. She was so persistent that she would require me to spend time in her office to perfect her course on property law. That was important. She took the time to teach and to inspire.

One of the greatest moments of my life was when she approached me and gave me a hug after I was presented with the University of Northern Kentucky Chase Exceptional Service Award in 2004.

Her caring and push for me to succeed are reasons why I chose to become a motivational speaker. She and other great teachers and mentors opened my eyes to the fact that I had the capacity to change in any positive way that I chose.

NKU is mostly a commuter school, but I found it was essential to live in a tiny single dorm room there to focus on my studies. My experiences at Notre Dame had taught me that was the best way to cut down on distractions. It was also a great way to get to know fellow students.

I needed a full focus of my life to get through there on a three-year fast track. Many students at Chase take a four-year track because they have families and need to work.

But I was in a hurry. That meant taking classes in the morning, a two-hour nap in the afternoon, and then using the rest of the day in the library. I didn't watch television and seldom went out with friends. That was the same formula that I used while sandwiching classes around football practices at Notre Dame.

The dorm life at Chase College of Law helped bring me in close contact with two dear friends—James Mathews and Brian Crutcher—who were deeply spiritual. We studied and debated and laughed a lot. We all served as officers of the Black Law School Association.

Humor was a big part of our lives as we dealt with the day-to-day stresses of law school. We'd also take time to ponder the bigger issues of life: how to be of service to others, how to help others make positive changes, and how to make the world a better place.

I made time to serve as president of the Black Law School Association. James and Brian served as officers too. That was a commitment akin to playing football at Notre Dame.

James and Brian are both amazing Christians. In fact, James is now a pastor at a church in Texas. We'd often sit and talk about classes. But the sessions would invariably lead into great discussions about interpreting the meaning of Christ in law and in life in general. They have enhanced my spiritual development. They modeled and supported what my mom had instilled in me.

One thing we quickly agreed upon was that we had to collaborate for a common cause. That's so important for life: to really have power, leaders have to win people over and build a consensus. We realized if we could lead our group, we needed to be strategic about it.

We decided in that sense that we would raise money professionally as opposed to piecemeal, because we had a positive message. We weren't going to spend a lot of time with bake sales, car washes, and other ways to get people together and raise bits of money. We simply had to be at another level of respect. We had to meet with presidents of companies and attend professional conferences. That's where we needed to spend our time to best represent black law students. That philosophy carries forward today in my role as CEO at Wernle Youth & Family Treatment Center. We have to think big in everything we do.

My development spiritually and educationally led me away from the sports-agent track I thought I was headed toward. I had worked the summer before graduating from law school for the sports marketing firm IMG. It was a great experience. I thought it would be great to stay in the world of athletics by representing young athletes. It was exciting, and I loved many aspects of it. I got close to the athletes and their families. I felt some of the same excitement that I'd enjoyed when being recruited.

But I couldn't move forward in that realm for several character-based reasons. For one, I didn't want to play games or use people. Sadly, that's how many agents land their clients. The young players (and often their families) were so focused on themselves and on making money. Some of them were immature, unmotivated, and had such unrealistic dreams. To succeed, I would have had to focus on their needs and build them up when at times I felt they needed a kick in the behind. I felt as if I'd need to compromise my morals to land some of the upcoming professionals. I just couldn't deceive anyone to enrich myself. They needed to be committed and work hard.

My morality and my values were worth far more than any amount of money I'd ever receive.

CHAPTER 12

Family Life

IT'S AMAZING TO think how many people lose opportunities that God put in front of them because their hearts aren't open or they just aren't focused on being friendly to others. There's never a reason not to be nice. My parents modeled that. Coaches Gerry Faust and Lou Holtz and Frank Eck and so many other mentors modeled that too.

Regis Philbin's amazing television career is based on a friendly persona, connecting with people in personal ways. He teases and pleases and also serves as the nation's good-morning advice dispenser. He can push powerful messages because he's popular yet so caring.

Leadership is modeled.

I learned that from watching my father being a leader at his business. I keep learning about leadership, too, by watching mentors and friends such as Leo Hawk, Dave DeVita, and Willis Bright. It's interesting; all of them are older and have such great senses of humor, of caring, and of commitment. They have so much power in wisdom and having lived what they preach.

If someone sees me as a physically imposing champion football player and says, "Wow, he's a powerful guy, yet all he thinks about is other people. He's spiritual and giving, a solid guy," well, how much more attractive would that make me?

Sad to say, but self-centeredness is a common trait for high-level athletes. It starts in high school and escalates like an explosion in college. There, players basically live a life of selfishness, even at a place like Notre Dame, where players live in the same dormitories and eat in the same cafeterias as every other student, where you are expected to do the same classwork as everyone else.

Being an athlete carries huge advantages while you are on a popular team. People want to do anything for you. Beautiful women want to be with you. Children and alumni want your autograph. You are treated like a king at parties.

In that kind of environment, no matter the university, kids are molded to be a receiver, not a giver. It cripples many of them. They can't adjust to the real world of work and relationships. That's the wrong campus environment. Healthy relationships just can't be as successful in a selfish environment.

The right environment is where you are pushed to make commitments to change, where there is a spiritual component. That makes you a better husband, a better father, and a better performer in your work career. You sacrifice what you are for what you want to become.

So many people go through life trying to get their partner to commit to them, and they don't know how to do it. You have to sometimes change the environment and get them to miss you. If he doesn't come after you, it wasn't meant to be.

Commitment is only the start. Changes are necessary throughout relationships.

Daily life can be tough. Raising kids is tough. Running a business is tough. My job demands that I be gone a lot. That is tough on my family

Christianity gives a foundation on how to live and raise kids successfully. The blueprint is in the Bible. I also have a real-life roadmap of what *not* to do by growing up in a broken home.

I had never seen a successful marriage. In that sense, some people could ask, "How could you expect to have a successful one?" Many young people blame themselves for their parents' breakups. There can be a lot of damage from that.

I ended up living with my mom, but my dad was an integral part of my success. He was responsible enough to move us to Hillside from Jersey City. We could have grown up in poverty. He was a workaholic, but he always came to pick my brothers and me up on weekends to join him at his shop.

It didn't work out for my mom and dad long-term, but he has been in a caring relationship for more than three decades with Diane Schwartz. That was hard to deal with for a long time because I was so close to my mother, and she had felt betrayed. But my dad's relationship models stability and commitment.

You can learn from the positives and negatives in life. You can watch and learn and see how other relationships are working. My parents never acted bitterly toward each other and always tried to do what was best for my sisters, brothers, and me.

Yes, you can lose perspective and lose your way. Children of broken marriages can feel abandoned and worry they may lack the ability to draw close to another adult in a balanced, healthy way. But you can learn how to balance things.

Dealing with broken relationships early in life can be a positive by making you see that you can change and that things can be better over time. If you never had a healthy relationship before, you have to change yourself. You have to be willing to let your parents be your resource. You have to realize the value of your partner's insights.

The first thing you have to do is to make sure you and your partner are first in your relationship. Talk to each other. If you have children, try to be good examples for your kids: happy, loving, focused, and disciplined. Find great joy in discovering what your partner wants and needs. Maybe you can't always be that person, but at least you know you will try to be a better partner and father.

The first step must always be to love your partner for who they are.

Then if you can't connect in some ways, you have to reevaluate. You have to put the focus back on you. I constantly ask myself, "Does what I am doing right now help me be a better parent? A better partner? A better boss?"

And when in doubt, consult a third party. I have sought out a counselor before because I wanted to learn how to communicate better.

Both parties have to agree on a change to make it work in a marriage. You have to work together to be successful. Communications and collaboration are essential in a strong relationship. People who succeed in life are good communicators. They work well together,

It's imperative in my realm to know how to write well and speak in public. I want to reach my full potential in my career, in my spiritual life, and in my relationship with my family. I center my decisions now on them.

Sometimes, it's more important to coach your child's basketball team than lead that committee or head out somewhere for a fun adult event. It's essential, I believe, to show commitment to your children. Be there to show you care and to push them to reach their potential.

Again, you need to have balance in your life as a family man and CEO. Now I can tell people who want my time, "Thanks for asking. I just can't make it this time. Ask me again, and we'll get together." Meetings can be rescheduled. There will be more golf tournaments and sports events to attend in the future. Friends, board members, and coworkers respect you for that.

It's important to realize that model works in 2017. It didn't as much thirty years ago, even twenty years ago. Fathers' priorities were more focused on their jobs. Society didn't allow them to be involved. Now our culture has changed. Taking time off is important today for a father. That's the way it should be.

One major thing that I pass on is a tribute to my father: self-sufficiency. You have to be willing to work hard and to listen to others to succeed. Your success comes down to you. Whenever Justis asks me a question, I turn it back on her and say, "Sweetie, you know how to find the answers." She will then head to a book or a computer and come back a little while later with the answer. It's kind of a game now. I want her to be independent, to find the answers for herself. Parents should sow seeds of success and give their children the tools needed to find the answers in their own lives.

I want my daughter to always have a goal in life. That goes for my son, Darrell Jr., too. They attend a Catholic school in Indianapolis. I believe in the educational mission of Catholic schools and the inclusiveness that allows students from other faiths.

I'd love for my children to follow me as students at Notre Dame. They certainly will be immersed in the campus culture with visits to South Bend, Indiana, several times a year. They know I stay in contact on a daily basis with friends, coaches, and teachers from there, and that the campus will always remain an immense part of my world. But they will make their own choices about the colleges they will attend. If it's meant to be, that's where they'll wind up. The important thing is that they read, study, and have a thirst to learn.

I want my children to know about justice. We chose the name Justis for our daughter because we wanted to set the bar high for her. We want her to know that she could become a lawyer or judge, possibly even the youngest ever Supreme Court justice. We want her to live a life of righteousness. To do that, we must model it.

We tell her every morning how she smart is. She has been getting all As in her classes. She takes that seriously. You have to tell kids—and keep telling them—that they are phenomenal human beings with potential and abilities. If no one tells them that, why should they believe it and achieve it?

I bring Justis to work every year on Martin Luther King Day when she's out of school. Children need to *see* leaders to *be* leaders. She already understands that she has the choice to be a leader or a follower.

My son is a born linebacker and a born leader. His motor never stops. He always wants to make the tackle, to carry the ball. I guess that's innate. You don't give 50 percent, 60, or 70; you give *everything.* Success comes from giving your all. It comes from making changes and defeating challenges.

I want my children and those who attend Wernle to know how to deal with pressure. Life is based on it. You can't crumble underneath it.

CHAPTER 13

NCAA to Wernle

DO YOU WANT to become a fantastic leader and future CEO? You can visualize it by simply substituting other positive words in the well-known acronym for *chief executive officer*. Try *character*, *excellence*, and *optimism*. Try *commitment*, *energy*, and *opportunity*.

Try being compassionate, ethical, and open-minded. You simply can't lose if you let those C-E-Os be your foundation toward leadership or toward making meaningful changes in your life. Coach Holtz preached it this way as the Irish built themselves into a national champion: Do the right thing. Do the best you can. Show you care. My dad and mom, as well as my great mentors and friends, always modeled the same positive things.

Most great leaders have outstanding character-driven qualities. But that doesn't mean they can't be tough and task-minded leaders like my dad, Lou Holtz, and Frank Eck. One football metaphor that relates to any business, educational institution, or charitable organization is "You have to build the right team to be a winner." You have to cut the folks who can't help your team, who can't follow your rules, or who don't fit in your plans. You have to make the tough decisions.

I was forced to make one about my career direction as I ended law school. I became focused on using my new analytical skills in case law to do the right things for others as well as for myself. I became focused on developing the character of young people. There was no better place to do that than with the NCAA. It was a natural progression for me to join the governing body and do-it-right leader for college sports.

The NCAA was starting new programs in educational and youth development. That was much better suited to my personality than working for a large law firm or as a sports agent. The latter two had much higher potentials for prestige and income. So did working on Wall Street, which had also been a long-held dream. There were good opportunities to join all three fields. Each was booming in the mid-1990s.

However, many things had changed for me as I advanced from Notre Dame into my first real job and then through law school. There had been the sudden deaths of loved ones, the compassionate leadership of mentors like Frank Eck, and the spiritual development I had undergone at law school.

So I signed on with the NCAA as a membership services representative. I knew they were moving into new headquarters when I did so. First, I worked in Kansas City, and then I moved to Indianapolis when the NCAA relocated there.

Fortunately, I had a friend at the NCAA, Kevin Lennon, whose father, Chuck, was at Notre Dame when I attended there. Chuck guided the Notre Dame Alumni Association as executive director for thirty years until retiring a few years ago. Both Kevin and Chuck model a caring personality and fierce loyalty. They both have an infectious spirit and always work to do what's right. That's amazingly important in their jobs.

Kevin has risen to become the vice president of Academic and Membership Affairs of the NCAA. He's always at the forefront of major eligibility issues, such as Cam Newton and the questions about how he ended up at Auburn. Auburn University and the NCAA enforcement staff conducted more than fifty interviews into whether Newton was paid to sign with Auburn. Kevin, along with others, would oversee the committee and governing process that would help make the determination in the Ohio State case that saw Terrell Pryor and four of his other teammates suspended the first five games for selling their memorabilia and eventually ended in the resignation of Coach Jim Tressel.

The NCAA offered a great environment for learning to lead. It was exciting as I was assigned to help pioneer the character-development and sportsmanship program called Stay in Bounds.

That role at the NCAA put me in touch with Willis Bright, another motivating and amazing person. He was the director of youth programs for the Lilly Foundation in Indianapolis. Willis always stands on the forefront of change in youth education. His main job is to determine whether organizations should be funded. It's a major part of his role to determine an organization's capacity to make the changes needed to make a program work.

My CEO spirit made me seek out Willis as a mentor when another friend and I were considering starting a business working with young people on character development. Willis laid out the possibilities perfectly and was very encouraging. He quickly became a caring and spiritual friend. He helped me see that successful changes build character and that there's no better feeling than watching someone grow along with you. Again, his advice harkened back to the qualities of the other career models in my life: stability, hard work, and care. All those qualities encouraged personal growth and change.

Besides looking at starting a character-development business, I wasn't looking for a major change outside of the NCAA. I loved that job, what it stood for, and its high profile across the country. But I must admit, I was intrigued when I first noticed an advertisement for the CEO job at Wernle.

I wanted to help young people and wanted to lead an organization. My life experiences had made me unfearful of a major change. Truth to tell, I knew nothing about Wernle until starting to research its mission and its long history. I was impressed that it was more than 120 years old and had a strong Christian-based (Lutheran) heritage.

Only one thing could've wrenched me away from the job at the NCAA—the chance to lead an organization that blended my skills with a great mission. It was a given that I needed experience as a leader if I was ever to become a CEO. But no matter what, I knew there was much to be learned from the interview process itself. It's funny to think about now, but what I learned first was rejection.

I felt confident that my first interview had gone well, but I wasn't hired. Wernle's interviewing team knew going in that I didn't have experience in the social services arena. But I wanted to expand my skill sets. I wanted to lead and be a CEO. However, I was told to develop more skills. How do you develop leadership skills without leading? Thousands who aspire big things face that same paradox every day.

I was frustrated, of course, but I consoled myself with the fact that I still had a great job at the NCAA—one that could put me on the fast track for becoming an athletic director at a university. I can remember thinking at the time that maybe I was meant to make my biggest impact at the NCAA, and I was perfectly fine with that. I was also committed to building Stay in Bounds, the character-development program that I had helped pioneer for the NCAA. We were now working with the NBA and NFL.

The CEO job just wasn't meant to be. Or so I thought.

But then, several months later, I got a call asking if I would consider the CEO job again at Wernle. Turns out, it just hadn't worked out with their first choice. It's amazing how often that happens. Many legendary coaches and leaders weren't the first choices either. But at first, I was inclined to say no. Simply put, I didn't like to lose at anything, and I had moved on in my mind. I would need some convincing.

The Wernle board chose Matt Gilmore of Celina, Ohio, the current board president, to reignite my interest in becoming CEO. We had forged one of those quick connections. In fact, he had voted to hire me originally. The vote was apparently very close.

Matt told me his wife refers to him as the consummate pessimist, but I was one of the handful of people in his entire life who had immediately gained his trust and respect. "You were absolutely magnetic, and we were all drawn to your strong personality," he says. "But recruiting you was no easy task. In fact, it was kind of a tortured path when I got drafted into trying to cajole you into taking the job. As you recall, we spent many, many nights talking on the phone, me preaching the good work at Wernle and you asking, 'Why should I take it?'"

But eventually, Matt convinced me, and I officially became a CEO. I knew I was up to the challenge.

I had a lot of catching up to do when I started on Wernle. One of the first things I needed was to obtain more education, specifically in strategic planning.

The business programs at Notre Dame and my work with Frank Eck gave me an awesome footprint for managing an organization. But law school was based in case law, not the day-to-day planning that I needed now on every level. So I applied and was accepted to the Harvard University program for strategic perspective in nonprofit management.

The program was comprised of all these business professionals and CEOs—men and women who were trying to get an edge in their fields. It was amazing. Here I was, at Harvard, a kid who had come from the streets of New Jersey to Notre Dame, to law school, and now to the university that carried the most prestigious name in the country. I was humbled.

The program brought in high-level people who analyzed making a complete change and developing strategies in respect to staffing, revenue generating, and holding people accountable.

I remember being impressed by the community-involvement mission of the company Timberland. The commitment began modestly with a request for the donation of fifty pairs of boots to the City Year program in Boston, Massachusetts. Now Timberland's Path of Service program offers employees forty paid hours for community service each year. It also offers six-month paid sabbaticals "to provide transformational service to non-profits, schools and community organizations."

President and CEO Jeff Swartz explained it this way: "At Timberland, we act on the belief that doing well and doing good are not separate activities. In fact, our commitment to social justice is a part of how we can earn our living. It's how we provide distinction for our customers. It's how we recruit top talent. Finally, it's how we create real, sustainable change in our communities and choose to compete in the world."

Timberland's commitment inspired more and more people and companies to start making good faith donations. It's amazing how great leadership can light that spark in people to help others.

The Harvard program made me start thinking about what great things could happen for Wernle and its residents and employees. I thought about how we could get bigger and better. I learned the best way to accomplish goals was by team building. We push strategies at Wernle. Everybody knows what's expected of them and is given the tools to be successful. We make sure everyone can reach their goals.

My education didn't stop at Harvard. Next, I completed a fundraising management program at the Indiana University School of Philanthropy. I also have earned certifications in leadership training, diversity training, and international public speaking.

I tried to help others to learn, too, on a collegiate level by serving as an adjunct professor of sports law at Ball State University. I speak a few times a month on a variety of topics: finding motivation and inspiration in these troubled times, developing the skills to become a strong leader, finding success through effective teamwork, dealing with adversity and overcoming life's challenges, developing successful youth and nurturing tomorrow's leaders, and enhancing your worth by developing strong character traits.

My continuing education and thirst for knowledge certainly helped transform me into a more effective leader. It's just like becoming a championship football player. You have to keep learning and practicing. You have to keep working out your mind and body. Then you have to perform when it really counts.

CHAPTER 14

The Wernle Story

THE BRIGHT LIGHTS that shine on my life now are the smiles of young people. Day after day, my victories are measured in lives changed, in successes attained, in positive outcomes.

Wernle Youth & Family Treatment Center is an amazing place. It treats more than one hundred residents every year. The lights that shine there are far more illuminating and more important than what goes on in any boxing arena, basketball court, or football stadium.

There are no bigger victories in life than helping change hurting children and their families. Children are scared and angry—hurting and confused—when they reach the rise in the rural road and first see our century-old historic brick building and campus.

By the time they leave, we want them to see the campus as the beacon of hope that it is—the spiritual light that points toward a better life.

The everyday problems most of us struggle with are nothing compared to what the young people at Wernle face. Our caring and talented staff fights deep psychological and societal issues every minute of every day. It's us against dysfunctional family issues, us against financial barriers, us against sexual deviancy.

Our residents are so vulnerable, so on the edge between living a life of incarceration or living a life of completeness. We give them hope. We educate them. We give them help with essential life skills. We give them a chance.

The best illustrations about the depth of work we do every day at Wernle come from those who see it from the outside in. We are accountable to the kids, their families, the state, our board, our donors, and our own tough internal criteria.

"One visit suggested to me that these boys were lost in the shuffle of life and how important my family was to me in having success in life," says Leo Hawk, a manufacturer and children's foundation leader from Lima, Ohio.

He and his family have been amazing benefactors for Wernle in the last several years.

"I admire that there are people like you and your team who give help before the kids are lost forever," Hawk said. "Wernle certainly is their last hope. It's the least we can do as brothers to help out."

Lou Holtz, who I have stayed in close touch with and as you know by now was my beloved coach on the last national championship team at Notre Dame, stated, "Wernle does some amazing things. There's no better cause than Wernle to help young people be successful. Their successes are a real tribute to the people who work there."

Father John Jenkins, the president of Notre Dame, noted the spirit of caring and learning that is obvious on our campus. "I have tremendous admiration for the work you are doing," he says. "It is tremendously challenging. It's a living testimony that everything counts. There are different kinds of education. It's about a transformation of a human being. It's about shaping souls."

Encouragement from my heroes means so much.

Any problems I've faced in my life or any accomplishment I've celebrated pale in comparison to the soul shaping that goes on every day at Wernle.

Let me tell you an amazing story about that. There is a former resident, a man in his early twenties, who lives in an apartment in Chicago. He has a job and a girlfriend. Things will never be perfect for him, but he has a positive direction in his life–one that we helped to shape.

We were able to help him with some serious issues several years ago at Wernle. It took hundreds of hours of therapy from our staff to draw him out and to help him gain the confidence to grow.

Our clinical director then was a wonderful man who died suddenly last fall at age seventy. He made a breakthrough when he discovered that the damaged young man had a tremendous knowledge of spiders. The young boy didn't fear them at all. In fact, he loved them and talked about them all the time. That was something highly unusual to the director, who had worked for decades in private practice as well as leading psychiatric services at top national hospitals.

The resident had studied spiders and knew how to identify dozens of different kinds by sight. He knew each one's traits. The clinical director learned why the resident was so fascinated with spiders as he sought to understand the severe social anxieties and damage he'd carried since childhood. The resident's mother had locked him in a closet while she was away at work when he was young. He was even put in the closet sometimes while she was home and didn't want to be "bothered."

This young man needed to find his own way of interacting, so the spiders had become his buddies. He would talk with them and hold them in his hands. He'd let them crawl all over him. Spiders became a normalcy in his abnormal environment.

That knowledge helped our clinical director bring up his own fascination with animals during their one-on-one discussions. The director's office was filled with photos and drawings of animals. A dog often sat in during his interview sessions. The connection helped lead to more understanding and much more successful treatment. The client's particular childhood trauma was truly unique, but not his situation.

Every child that comes to Wernle has faced a trauma that is unique to him or her. They have all experienced a great deal of loss and grief. They aren't really being rehabilitated, the clinical director pointed out. "We are 'habilitating.' We are helping them find what they've missed most." In this instance, the boy missed out on so many forms of what is considered regular childhood relationships in nurturing environments. He had no playmates. His playground was a claustrophobic closet filled with spiders.

As the CEO, I know that we can't undo all the damage of a lifetime, but we do everything that we can to help a young person in eight or nine months. Some of our residents have been through a dozen or more foster homes and social service agencies. It's foreign to many of the young men in those kinds of situations to form bonds with people and to form trusting relationships.

They've spent their lives scared, anxious, and not knowing what will happen next. Moral development for many of them was stunted at an early age, so they have problems understanding right and wrong. They've had a tough time just surviving. But that essentially is what they are great at. They have learned how to survive and adapt with what they have been presented.

Dozens of young men find their ways to positive and productive lives every year through the help of our committed staff at Wernle. We rank at the top in many categories for residential care in the state of Indiana.

Here are some numbers:

- 89 percent of our discharges were planned. The state average was 72 percent.
- 71 percent of our discharged residents were reunited with families. The state average was 50 percent.
- Nearly nine out of ten of our residents have obtained positive education outcomes at discharge. That is reflected in a campus-wide rise in GPAs to 3.0 from 2.0.
- Our family satisfaction level was 6.5 on a scale of 7. The state average was 6. It is essential to our program to treat families as well.

By the way, there are many other great facilities. If a young man or woman can't get the best help here, we want him to find it somewhere else.

Sometimes the positive effect isn't immediate. We have received touching letters or emails several years after working with young people. They often talk of how people cared at Wernle, sometimes detailing what we might think is the smallest thing or have long forgotten.

We often make a difference quickly, but sometimes it doesn't even show before the young men move on to the next stations in their lives, hopefully rebuilding relationships with their families. "We'll hang in there as long as we can. I want them to know we're still there and we care," our then-clinical director said. "Somewhere down the line, something you said or did clicks and has an impact you didn't know."

For example, one resident left Wernle without noticeable changes many years ago. He needed other services, which even included time in jail. The resident kept in contact with our clinical director and always remembered the caring treatment he received at Wernle. They formed a bond that lasted. After leaving jail, he has made an amazing turnaround. He has a job and has forged some important relationships in his life. "The Department of Corrections never thought he'd see the light of day," said Wernle's clinical director. "But we attended his wedding. That is very satisfying."

Positive outcomes are the ultimate goal at Wernle. We aim to build relationships and instill confidence. It sometimes takes months just to discover how to help residents begin to change and to restore their damaged lives. It starts with hope. It's mandatory that our staff and I have the same belief: *children are our most precious product.*

Our jobs are focused on treating them in a safe and secure environment. My role is to make it easier for staff members to focus on that treatment. I need to give them the tools to do their jobs by dealing with the administrative issues. That means I am often away, attending statewide conferences, board events, and one-to-one conferences.

A major part of my role is building relationships and raising funds to help us grow. Our small development department mirrors that effort. We keep in contact with hundreds of Lutheran churches, hundreds of businesses, and thousands of individuals.

The efforts get more intense every day as governments have slashed their payments and businesses, and individuals battled through the long economic downturn and recovery. Wernle's philosophy has been to work closely with governmental bodies and our donors. We believe that by proving results, we will grow. We don't waste time complaining about cutbacks. We learn what those who make the decisions are looking for and how we can complement one another and work together toward a common goal.

I was attracted to Wernle at first because its mission was to help heal kids, but Wernle needed some healing too. Wernle needed a new focus just to survive. It desperately needed leadership in an ever-evolving environment. I believed my skill sets as a strategist, lawyer, and motivator offered a unique fit. I had experiences dealing on a regional and national level with Notre Dame and the NCAA.

Change isn't easy for people or organizations. But you simply must embrace it. The rules, regulations, and funding structures are constantly changing. For example, cash-strapped state hospitals and juvenile facilities have toughened up standards for admitting young people and the focus is on getting them back with their families quicker.

The result? We are dealing at Wernle with young men and women with deeper psychological and behavioral problems. We are dealing with increasingly tougher issues and backgrounds. The kids are more severely damaged. They've all been abused and neglected. They have a hard time trusting adults and have a propensity to lash out.

Just like I'd found at the other campuses of my life, it was essential for me to focus on education and a purpose-driven life, as well as the underlying issues that were requiring therapeutic help.

Our program teaches confidence, faith, and self-reliance. Lots of us should be thankful that our circumstances didn't require us to need residential care. These kids are certainly troubled, but truly amazing. Contrary to many beliefs, there are honor students among them. They want to achieve positive things. One of our residents was invited to attend an exclusive summer program at Georgetown University. Most of our former residents have gotten a high school diploma or GED. Many are attending college. We had dozens make the honor roll each year in the local school system.

Those are all miracles in many ways, considering many of the residents have faced unimaginable abuse and neglect in their lifetimes. Following are some amazing facts about young people who needed residential care services in Indiana in the last five years:

- Each child had an average of 4.53 prior placements. This is a reason why we consider ourselves a last chance at hope.

- 55.77 percent had been a witness to domestic violence.
- 51.92 percent had a history of special education.
- 50 percent had parents with a history of incarceration.
- 48.08 percent had suffered from physical abuse.
- 46.15 percent had a history of neglect.
- 28.85 percent had experienced some form of sexual abuse.

As one example of a strategic goal, we made a commitment to boost our residents' collective grade point average to 3.0. It was 2.0 at the time, so we would be improving by 50 percent. It took eighteen months to reach that goal (over three semesters), and we've seldom deviated much from that number despite always dealing with new residents.

I make a personal vow to all residents that I will take everyone who earns 4.0 GPAs in a semester to lunch at the restaurant of their choice. Those lunches truly are special times. We talk and learn more about each other. My credit card takes a quite a big hit thanks to their healthy appetites for steaks and seafood at Red Lobster, their restaurant of choice, but it's worth it!

The students are always so proud. It's amazing what I learn and how similar their goals are to kids who are in more traditional settings. Our residents have just experienced so many more negatives in their young lives. Each one could be a budding scientist, chef, or businessman. Some won't advance that far. Some will unfortunately end up in prison despite our best efforts. But we will never stop trying to help them when they are with us.

Dave Eggen/Inertiasports.net

CHAPTER 15

Wernle Keeps Changing

WERNLE WAS SURVIVING month to month when I came here in 2001 after working four years with the NCAA. The 72-acre campus is beautiful, with a pastoral, tranquil environment. Big rolling fields and large trees surround the facility on the southeastern edge of Richmond, Indiana.

I remember the first day on campus like it was yesterday. We were fourteen residents under census and a loss then of about $1 million a year. Current assets were only $240,000 more than our liabilities. We had no savings and no strategic plan for the future. Our staff was unlicensed, and our program was unaccredited. With a lack of commitment and structure, we were headed to probation with the state licensing agency that supervises treatment centers for youth. That meant we weren't high on the list for getting new clients—the young people and their families that we are designed to help, the lifeblood of our success.

As a detail-focused strategist, I figured that we needed to first tackle some basics, such as marketing, public relations, and programming. We also desperately needed to focus on developing new sources of financing. The perception of Wernle wasn't good in Richmond and the immediate area. The donor base was dwindling. There was a revolving door of employees. There was no coordinated way to attract residents. We were just taking what came. We needed to focus on building a more contemporary and challenging program—one that was well respected in the community, the state, and around the nation. We needed to focus on a client base that we could help. To do all those things, we needed to make some quick and drastic changes.

One simple but vital change was to rebrand the institution from Wernle Children's Home to Wernle Youth & Family Treatment Center. Wernle started as a Lutheran orphanage in the decade after the Civil War, and the name hadn't changed despite the changes in services focused on troubled children.

The only way to deal with a huge problem is to change the landscape and the mind-set of people. For me, that meant hiring a completely new executive staff who would embrace a new vision and mission for Wernle. We accomplished that quickly, but it took time to build trust with the agencies that send the boys. They have choices about where to place them.

Simply put, we have made quantum leaps.

Following are some examples of financial changes from 2001 to 2016:

Current assets have risen from $1,843,308 to $9,122,657.

Net assets have risen from $3.76 million to over $14 million.

Liabilities have fallen from $1.6 million to $826,972.

Property and equipment have risen from $3.46 million to over $6 million.

We're now on a far stronger footing and are preparing for the future. As of 2016, Wernle is a thirteen-million-a-year business that serves an average of about one hundred boys and girls each year in residential care. The numbers are far higher when you add in the children and their families that we service with our new outpatient care. We have worked hard to convince people that we are an economic development engine in Wayne County, where we are located. We spend nearly $2 million a year with local vendors. Our employment numbers are rapidly rising. We employed 90 in 2012. That number grew to 120 in 2013, 140 in 2014, and we expected to have 170 plus in 2017. That number makes Wernle a top 20 employer in the county.

How are we doing it? We have built our donor base and our positive relationship with the Indiana Department of Children's Services. The latter relationship alone resulted in a $1.4 million grant in 2014 to add forty staff jobs. They included a staff psychologist, eight nurses, seven program managers, a trainer (who will lead our new leadership institute), and numerous direct-care staff.

We then received an additional $700,000 from the DCS to boost salaries to match statewide averages. Nearly every employee received a pay increase of at least $2 per hour. That has resulted in more job applicants and more qualified candidates.

Each program is staffed by a team of highly trained and dedicated professionals, including therapists, youth counselors, medical professionals, a campus chaplain, and many more support and administrative professionals.

We finished a $10 million campaign to replace buildings and institute new programs that will help us reach young people for another century. Through this effort, we built a new girls' unit and a residential sex offenders' unit, plus we refurbished our Wellness Center, all at the cost of more than $2 million. We also finished construction on another residential unit ($2 million) in 2017 and a new administration building ($3 million) in 2018. We also secured $1.5 million for our endowment to ensure sustainability so we can help young people for another century.

We are evolving every day into new areas, as we must. We have plans to start an outpatient drug-addiction program that is focused on helping young boys and girls from around eastern Indiana. That type of service is increasingly needed as states cut back on more expensive residential programs. Parents or caretakers can self-refer their children for services from around the region.

Besides the facilities mentioned above, we have added home and community-based services. We built apartments so parents could visit their children without incurring large hotel bills. We also provide transportation to our residents and their families. We have new computerized programs for Medicaid billing and health records.

Our focus is to help build the young person's confidence and behavioral controls so they can live at home or in a less restrictive environment. For some of the kids, Wernle represents their last and best hope of acceptance and assistance. So we take our role very seriously.

We have succeeded in developing a businesslike management structure. Now one major question is, How can we sustain our competitive nature? If I do it, I want to be the best at it. I expect the same of my employees. We are developing strategic plans each year to thrive. We constantly focus on and push strategies. Everybody knows expectations and how to complete them.

As I previously mentioned, I went back to campus to learn more about management—a strategic planning program at Harvard that gave me great insights into many sides of successful business models. All these business professionals and CEOs were there, trying to get an edge.

They brought in high-level people who analyzed complete change as major strategies. The classes intensely focused on ways to develop staffing, generate revenues, and hold people accountable in every role.

We are looking decades down the line at Wernle, not just at survival for another year. We *will* be here for the long-term. It's likely that many other similar places that are struggling won't be around. We could merge or join forces to better serve the state.

What separates our facilities from most others is that we take a holistic approach. We educate our residents and offer them therapeutic services. We work with families as well as teachers, doctors, and judges. We are also evolving into an educational setting. Wernle has hired an education director and has been provided teachers by the local school system to further improve outcomes with our residents.

Our campus is changing every day. Our residents are changing. I am changing. Our mission is adjusting and thriving in a constantly shifting environment. We can never stray from our core values and must always remain focused on being stewards today and in the future.

Funding is tight. Personal and corporate donations are harder to get. Donors hold us accountable. They want to make sure we are providing quality care. It's different from the past. People are now saying, "Show me outcomes." Our board is holding us accountable. We have matrix and systems in place that weren't available in the past to monitor outcomes.

The state holds us increasingly accountable and is constantly looking for ways to slash costs. We are getting more clients with increasingly serious cases. But we welcome the challenge. I'm excited every day about where we are going on this campus of my life. I think each day at work, *What can we do today to make this a better place? What can I do to make that happen?*

One of the best ways is to be a campus of change. A campus is a family, a helping hand, a disciplinarian, a direction. I realize that I would not be working as Wernle's leader without experiencing other campuses as launching pads to excellence.

It's been a progression of learning, with special coaches and teachers, hard-driving friends and fellow students, and advice-offering alumni and mentors. Every valuable lesson has helped me to build a team and an atmosphere at Wernle that has taken us from near ashes to standing as one of the most respected residence homes in the Midwest. Education at Wernle is for the employees as well as the young residents. It is about making positive changes, paying attention to details, and moving in new directions.

Our therapeutic treatment programs focus on the strengths of individuals rather than their failures. Our ultimate goal is simple: provide the tools for a better future by treating them with dignity, integrity, and care.

A recent resident named offers testimony to the effect we are having. He has turned his life around amazingly. He is studying to become a nurse. He performs missionary work and often visits Wernle to speak to the boys about the changes in his life and the opportunities that will be available to them after successfully completing our treatment program.

His journey and the journeys of hundreds of others inspire us to keep improving every day.

CHAPTER 16

Tragedies

OFTENTIMES, MAJOR CHANGES are forced upon us because of pain. It can get so bad that you simply have to change to survive. You have to get a new job after you get laid off or fired. You have to reflect on yourself and change to revive or end a failing relationship.

The possibilities are endless. The death of a loved one demands change. A near-death experience demands it. Experiences like these demand that you grow, adjust, and fall back on others for help.

The brightest days of my life have been tempered by tragedy.

Death can strike at any time, adding an emotional toll that shakes you to the soul, that puts the sleepless in your nights, that puts you on bended knee in front of God. It's as if He reaches down to touch the go-go-go soul with a stop sign. He lets us know who's in control and gives us an unwanted and unexpected jolt.

I'm certainly a living example that success and sorrow often stand side by side in this life. They are the ultimate change makers. I've had my share of jolts, the deaths of special people in my life, and some near-death experiences too.

My wonderful sister Charnette died when I was just hitting my stride at Notre Dame. A close Irish teammate, Bob Satterfield, collapsed and died at my feet just hours after the Irish celebrated our championship at the White House. My mother then passed away suddenly just as I was embarking on the huge challenge of law school.

The deaths also include a seventeen-year-old nephew who was shot to death—the victim of senseless gang violence in New Jersey. Just recently, a young man died in a drowning accident while attending Wernle Youth & Family Treatment Center.

Each tragedy prepared me a bit more to face up to the others.

There were close calls, too, with death that could easily have inalterably changed the destiny of a national championship in the 1988 season.

Those situations never really hit the headlines: a jet carrying the whole team home from the season finale against Miami in 1985 came within seconds of crashing at the South Bend Airport during a blinding snowstorm. I thought we were going to die. A few teammates and I also survived a car accident early one morning after we had been out together before a bowl game.

Each experience tempered my quest for success yet drove me at the same time.

Charnette's death shook me up like no other event in my life. She was so full of energy, so full of goodness. She was literally ripped from me before she was even thirty.

Charnette suffered so much, I learned later, as I was fighting tooth and nail just to pass the first year at Notre Dame. I redshirted because of an injury, and uncertainty surrounded my role. I was concentrating so much on my own experiences, my own college survival, that I wasn't aware of the tragedy that was unfolding at home in New Jersey.

Then Charnette died.

I knew she had been battling a lingering illness for some time, but I had no idea that it was life-threatening. In fact, she brought several friends to a Notre Dame game at the Meadowlands in my freshman year, and everyone had a great time. She smiled so much that day and kept telling me how proud she was, and our family was, that I could make it at a place like Notre Dame.

It was evident during the last times we saw each other a bit—in the summer before—that she was having issues with nausea and breathing. She'd be sick and coughing and then run to the bathroom and throw up.

The last time I remember seeing her, during Christmas break, she appeared fine—her happy self. I came to find out later from our parents that she'd had heart complications when she was young, but they hadn't wanted to burden us with that news at such a young age. It became more and more of a challenge for her to breathe in the last years.

Dad would take her to the doctor, and they could never get a grasp on how to deal with the problem that she presented. As time progressed, it just kept getting worse. Her heart wasn't pumping out with the volume that it needed. Finally, they put her into intensive care as her body simply shut down.

They could just not figure out what was going on with her heart. She just had grown weaker and weaker. My father told me to come home, and I just made it to see her still alive. I walked in, and my whole family was there—Mom, Dad, siblings, and cousins. She was already in a coma.

I honestly didn't understand the complete gravity of the situation as I flew home. They just said she was sick. There certainly was a part of the situation where I didn't want to know or didn't want to speculate. There's just no way that you want to believe that your vibrant, compassionate sister is terminally ill.

I started to suspect something horribly bad was happening when a cousin picked me up at the airport, and she didn't share a lot as we went directly to the hospital. My parents knew how hard I was trying to make it at Notre Dame, so they didn't want to bother or worry me. They shielded me. That was possible then because I called home only once or twice every couple of weeks. South Bend is nearly seven hundred miles away.

After finally arriving at the hospital, I experienced one of the most vivid scenes of my life—something I still have nightmares about today. I walked up the stairs and turned down the corridor toward the waiting room. My mom and dad were sitting together, holding each other for the first time I can remember since their marriage had broken up. They saw me and started to cry. That was so traumatic for me.

I knew then that something horrible was happening to our family.

Thankfully, I was able to see Charnette while she was still breathing. She was in a coma and died within hours. It was a blur through the funeral. I hardly remember anything from the next week or so. I'll wish forever that I had more time to spend with her.

Chris was at home during that year and had more insight on it. The impact was huge on his life. He recalls, "We think she contracted something from the times she was visiting Nigeria with a friend. The science wasn't as good in the 1980s as it is now. It attacked her immune system, and they couldn't figure it out. It was up and down until the end. She looked very normal, and it never was drawn out. But she went into a coma and then died. She was such a sweet person. It was such a shock."

It's still a mystery what killed Charnette. I can speculate that the cause was something that she caught—like the flu, pneumonia, or an infection—that aggravated her underlying heart and breathing issues. My family chose not to have an autopsy done. I'm not certain that was the best decision because her overriding illness could have been hereditary. How do I know that it won't strike my children or my nieces and nephews?

I've always wondered if she had best doctors and wondered if her death really was just inevitable. But speculating doesn't really matter. God puts people here on earth for a short time. When He calls you, it's time to go.

The only thing I could do after her death was pray and promise to emulate her goodness throughout the rest of my life. There wasn't a day that went by in college that I didn't get down on my knees and pray for her and thank her for guiding me so much. I feel like her spirit stood over me as I progressed through Notre Dame.

There's a story involving her death that tells so much about my father. He wanted me to come home immediately, which wasn't easy at that time. His efforts made him reach out to the president of Notre Dame. My dad said he would pay the university back if it would make the arrangements for me to fly back. Notre Dame made that happen. For all I know, the president put the flight on his credit card. I'm pretty sure, though, that he was surprised to get the money back so soon. My dad sent the check back with me when I returned to school. I was shocked that he had no qualms about going to the top to get what he desired. That takes guts and ability.

My father always had a knack for communicating, getting his point across, with anybody. His friends include janitors, neighbors, street people, and bank presidents. He wasn't afraid to reach out and ask for help. And he's also willing to give it. He also follows through on his promises. All those attributes rubbed off on me, as did Charnette's.

I plan someday to honor her legacy by starting a scholarship fund in her name so other women will have the chance to have wonderful campus experiences. I think it will be for first-time college attendees and for women who work hard but don't have the finances to get to college on their own.

When I get in tough spots at times, I just take a break in my mind and think back on her smile, her humor, her inner beauty, and the positives she brought to life.

The thoughts never fail to bring me peace.

I miss so much just talking with her. She was always an inspiration.

My memories of her prove again and again that God's love always shines through.

God's love shone through my mom's health problems too. As I previously shared, she died soon after I started to attend Chase College of Law at University of Northern Kentucky. I didn't know how tough it would be academically there. It's amazingly ironic that another tragedy struck while I was stretching every academic ability that I possessed.

My mom had come to live with me in Cincinnati after suffering a severe heart illness. I had rushed back to Hillside after an aunt called and said Mom wasn't doing well. Her condition was worse than I imagined as I drove home to New Jersey. For those who know me, it's probably no surprise that was one fast trip. I have a heavy foot on the accelerator, and I worried the whole way. God was with me because I didn't get a ticket or cause an accident.

When Mom came to the door of her apartment to greet me, she looked severely ill. I remember her being so tall and energetic throughout my school years. This time, she was so bloated. She was filling up with fluids and had a hard time drawing a breath. She was acting very confused. Of course, she said she was just fine. But she wasn't.

I collapsed in tears at the sight of my mom in such obvious weakness and distress. She didn't want to go to the hospital, but I insisted. "We need to go. *Now.*"

The gravity of the situation was conclusively proven when she was rushed in for emergency treatment just a few moments after a clerk asked for her insurance cards at the hospital. Mom was in the midst of congestive heart failure. Suddenly, I saw many nurses and doctors run into this room with her. The doctors said later that she definitely could have died if we'd waited only a few hours more to get to the hospital.

Her condition made me realize immediately that she needed day-to-day attention—something I felt responsible for providing. I had left a decade before to find myself, and she'd always encouraged me. It was my turn to take care of her.

It was impossible for any of my siblings to take over that duty. Brother Chris was away at Brown University, and Charnette had passed away by then.

My two older brothers were facing life issues that precluded them from providing the daily help my mom needed. It was one of the most challenging experiences I've ever faced. My life had changed in a matter of hours.

I felt responsible for my mom's survival. I knew that she needed to be with me in Cincinnati. So I made the decision to have her come there to live with me in my two-bedroom apartment in a complex I had purchased. I'm so grateful that could happen. We had a great eight months together.

My life took a conflicting turn a couple months after her arrival. I received a letter informing me that I was accepted into Chase College of Law at University of Northern Kentucky. At first, I thought there was no way I could do it. It was my dream, but I had a great job, owned an apartment complex, and of course, had my mom living with me.

It was a time in my life I had to make critical decisions.

Mom said she was so proud that I was accepted to Chase and that it was destiny for me to go even if it meant we'd be apart for substantial periods of time again. (I'd need to live in the dorms in order to give it my 100 percent focus.) Mom simply didn't want to hear that it wasn't the right time for me to go because of her illness. It was the natural, God-inspired process, she said, just like when she and Dad moved from South Carolina to find a better life.

I made arrangements for a nurse to visit her twice a week, but I didn't know her time left was so short. I saw her several times a week and was so glad to have her so close by.

One day, a dean called me into her office and said I needed to go immediately to a hospital in Cincinnati. She wouldn't tell me why, but in my heart I knew the inevitable. When I got there, a doctor said my mom had died from a heart attack.

It was a comfort to know that she had just seen a doctor for a cardiac checkup and was leaving the office when she collapsed. There was nothing that could have been done. She didn't suffer. God had simply called her home.

It turned out to be one of the most impactful and educational months of my life.

Even though her death came at an unexpected time, I had immediate closure because we had so many special moments in her final months. I am so thankful for that. I hadn't been around her much in the previous decade, so it was such a blessing to take her under my wing, to laugh and hug and share stories.

I had realized how much at peace she was with her life and the possibility of death. Her main focuses in life were her family and her church. She was so strong in her faith every day. She preached that we should celebrate life achievements—and celebrate death too—and to go out and make a better world. I honor her every day by doing so.

Bob Satterfield's death touched everyone affiliated with the Irish. One moment we were out celebrating a visit to the White House in the afterglow of our national championship, and the next a popular player was dead.

Bob, Mark Green, and I were simply socializing at a nightspot in Michigan that was just across the border from Indiana and only about five miles from campus. None of us were heavy partiers. In fact, I don't remember any of us drinking alcohol that night. We were really straight guys, never in any trouble. We avoided anything that would cast a negative light on the university or ourselves. But this was a huge night to celebrate. We were so happy and were having a good time. We had met President Reagan earlier that day as the national championship team. It was his last day in office. None of us had ever met a president before, much less been in the White House.

Bob had just been dancing and appeared to be feeling just fine. He was talking and laughing before suddenly passing out and falling to the ground. I actually thought he was joking around. Then he went into convulsions.

Help arrived fairly quickly, but it was obvious something was seriously wrong. They worked on him so long in the ambulance before they even headed for the hospital. He apparently had been treated before for a congenital heart problem. We found that out afterward.

I remember telling Mark to hurry as we followed the ambulance in his car. But Bob was pronounced dead soon after arriving at the hospital in South Bend. It was so surreal and so unexpected when we were told that Bob had died.

It was so ironic too. His death occurred early Inauguration Day morning for President George Bush in 1989.

Bob had worked so hard in his home area of Southern California for the chance to attend Notre Dame. He had lived the dream of being a college football player and made it to the top of the mountain with the Irish.

It was so impressive because he made the team as a walk-on. Not many people get the chance to play on a title team and meet the president. I don't know of any who died just hours afterward.

I can only imagine the great things he would have accomplished if he had lived.

It was such a shock and something that has driven me to show people they can overcome nearly anything. Your life is your most precious commodity. Make every hour count.

Your life changes when you witness things like Bob's collapse or see your sister's life robbed by a fatal illness. You realize anybody can die at any moment. One of the biggest lessons to learn from the death of a close relative or friend is to make the change that you want now. You never know what tomorrow will bring, or even if it will come.

Coach Holtz told Mark and me soon after Bob Satterfield's death that when he got the phone call, he knew the circumstances couldn't be mischievous because we were the ones with him when he collapsed. That means a lot to me. People notice how you live your life. Coach Holtz drew comfort from the way we were.

Coach Holtz proved how much Bob's life and death mattered by canceling plans to attend the inauguration so he could immediately return to South Bend.

Notre Dame helped Mark and myself recover from the shock by contacting the NCAA to see if we could represent the institution by serving as pallbearers for his funeral. (The NCAA considers an institution paying for flights for student athletes to attend a funeral a violation of NCAA rules and regulations unless a waiver can be granted.) It really was a tough time, but the NCAA granted our waiver. Bob's family was so thankful we could be there.

I was thankful too. We were honored to be pallbearers. The support from Notre Dame and Bob's family was so instrumental in dealing with the death and in gaining closure.

Thinking recently about Bob's death made me remember another incident that could have been catastrophic. It would have inalterably affected the school, the football team, and hundreds of families.

The Irish were returning deep in the night from a game at Miami in my sophomore year. It was the last game before Coach Gerry Faust announced he was stepping down. Most of the players were sleeping. The wind was howling, and snow was pouring down as the jet approached South Bend's airport.

The turbulence was strong.

The jet with at least one hundred players, coaches, and supporters had just touched down when I heard someone scream, "Pull up, pull up!"

The jet did just that, shooting toward the sky again. Most of the players didn't even know what happened and how close we had come to dying.

I can't remember whether the warning came from the cockpit or someone else looking out the window. But apparently, the airport hadn't been cleared enough of the ice and snow. We could have overshot the runway and hit something. We all could have been killed, just like the accident that decimated the whole team at Marshall University in the 1970s.

The Notre Dame jet was diverted to Chicago, where we took a bus back to campus. It took an extra three hours, but I didn't care.

In my dreams sometimes, I can still see this surreal snowy scene and feel the turbulence of that jet. It's amazing to think of the what-ifs: I wouldn't be here. My kids wouldn't be here. The history of Notre Dame football would have been changed forever. Many players on that jet were instrumental in winning the national title.

I am just so thankful that story had a happy ending. God was indeed protecting our plane that night.

Earlier, I alluded to a disaster avoided by the Irish before a game during my career. Many of us, including all-Americans, did something stupid early one morning and nearly got ourselves killed or arrested.

We were with a group that closed the bar the morning. We were in a warm-weather city before a game. We were having fun, and several had been drinking. Six of us all crammed in a little Chevette or some kind of rental car that size.

I don't know why I got in that car. All of a sudden, before I knew it, we were driving the wrong way down a one-way street and swerved to miss another car that was heading right at us. We did a 360, hit the curb, and tipped over. We came to rest right side up.

I really thought we were going to die as the car spun. Instead, the only problem was a flat tire and some very scared young men. No sooner had we gotten the tire fixed and the car back on the road than a police car turned onto the road along with us. What if he had been on the road when we spun out? The guys all knew how fortunate we were. That was pure luck, or God was looking over us that night. One second later, and we would have been in big trouble. Of course, that was minor compared to the possibility that many of us could have died or been seriously injured. Thankfully, tragedy was avoided that night. Many of us went on to play and win a national championship.

CHAPTER 17

Changes in a FLASH

TO MAKE A major change happen, people must have the ability to do so.

They must be able to make the necessary adjustments to sacrifice what they are for what they want to become.

Nearly four decades of changes—some very significant—have proven that to me. I'd like to offer some insights into how to make a positive change in your life by using examples from critical points in my own life story.

This will hopefully help you to recognize similarities in your own life and to navigate through the different campuses, the different situations, in your life to achieve the goals you desire. Those critical moments helped me to devise the change method I call FLASH points.

Change isn't always easy or quick, but the FLASH points offer an accumulation of ideas and guidance I've received from some dedicated and successful people.

They are examples that provide a map for transformation. They've worked for me. I'm confident they will work for you.

The first step is this:

1. Face up to change.

Wanting to change simply isn't enough. It's the starting point. Those desiring to transform themselves must know they can do so. They must be confident in themselves. Just arriving at that conclusion could take a lot of soul-searching, a lot of self-awareness, and a lot of trial and error.

I will emphasize the good news: you can do it. It's very important that you make a calculated effort to initiate change. Ask these kinds of questions of yourself: Are you satisfied with where you are in life? How badly do you want—or need—to change?

What do you really want to do with your life? How would a drastic change affect those around you? Those are important questions because studies show there is a big gap between how people perceive themselves and how they really are when it comes to being proactive about change.

This is the second step:

2. Learn your capacity to change.

To be honest, many people don't feel they possess the capacity to change for a variety of reasons. Some fear it. Some fight it because it invades their comfort zones. Some deny it; they simply don't see a reason to change.

But I believe the great majority has the capacity to change. Many people simply haven't been presented with the necessary tools to transform themselves.

Those tools will naturally lead to the third step:

3. Adopt a plan of action.

So many efforts to change are unsuccessful—and so frustrating—because the path isn't clear. It doesn't matter where you get started on your personal plan. Solicit advice from a family member, a friend, a minister, a teacher, a doctor, or someone else you trust and admire. Seek guidance from books, pamphlets, and articles. Check out programs offered by businesses, schools, medical establishments, and many more organizations.

Start by outlining your plan with identifiable achievement steps over a six-month period. Why six months? Well, it takes about six months on average to cement a major change. That means there is a lot of in-between time when commitment and perseverance are essential.

The in-between time is perhaps the most critical of all. Doubts creep in. Past failures can weigh on your mind. "It's not so much that we're afraid of change or so in love with the old ways, but it's that place in between that we fear," said famed author and speaker Marilyn Ferguson. "It's like being between trapezes. It's Linus when his blanket is in the dryer. There's nothing to hold on to."

In this in-between time, a support system is crucial, which brings us to the critical fourth step:

4. Secure a support system.

Studies have shown that 80 percent of the American people never change until they experience a severe degree of discomfort. The remaining 20 percent are proactive and thus are the most successful in our country. A strong network is essential in helping you move past the usual 80 percent failure rate for major changes. In fact, it could play the most critical role for success.

There is nothing you want to change that hasn't been accomplished before. There are people who want you to succeed and are willing to help you do it.

Support helps you build the courage to make changes. It helps you when you want to pull away, when the pressure grows. That's especially true when there are major barriers to be overcome. And there's no doubt that most monumental changes have barriers.

The fifth and final step is this:

5. Hold on to change.

You have to embrace your change and find a way to hold on. You have to ride it to success. So much of the change process is learning to discipline yourself. That's possibly the most important ingredient to succeeding on any level. Simply put, you have to work hard for any major success.

Since my teenage years, I've been able to focus on what's been needed at the time to advance me to the next level of life. That comes in part from an innate drive, a fear of failure, the ability to push myself, and the acceptance that others may need to push me.

I don't believe in mediocrity and won't accept it. People should push themselves to reach the height of their abilities. You can complete your change and move on to another. You can be an example to others.

Taking Action

Now that you know the FLASH points, how can you use them to your advantage? It's easier than you think. Here's how I put FLASH points into action at three crucial points in my life to achieve success.

High school challenge: Spurned at first by Notre Dame because of academic inadequacies.

I was an outstanding football player in high school, and many colleges took notice. Most major universities sent a coach to my school, who made a big show of meeting me and my high school coaches. However, the Notre Dame representative didn't even take the time to talk to me. One of my favorite sayings is that major changes often happen only after undergoing a significant degree of discomfort.

I have felt the severe discomfort many times, none more so than at this critical point in my life. This is the single most profound event that propelled me onto the path that I took. Here's how FLASH points helped me triumph in this "make it or break it" moment in my life.

Face up to change.

1. I acknowledged to myself and to others that I would do anything necessary to get into Notre Dame.

2. I was simultaneously embarrassed and motivated by Notre Dame's snub. I didn't make it personal. Pain is an amazing stimulant for positive change.

3. I knew immediately that I needed to make better decisions and work harder on my academics.

Learn your capacity to change.

1. I always had good discipline, so I called on that power.

2. I was the strongest player on my high school team. If I could commit myself to bench press twice my body weight, I could commit myself to getting better grades. I used pride as a powerful stimulant for changing my behavior.

3. When I compete, I always want to win. This was a battle. I would have to prepare like I did in every sport I played.

Adopt a plan of action.

1. Cut down on distractions. That meant refusing the temptations to stay out late and party. Do this just as you would cut down on costs when financial times are tough.

2. Focus on getting better grades and scoring high on tests. Study at home and especially in study hall. Stop playing cards and shooting the breeze in classes.

3. Communicate desires to teachers, coaches, and family.

Secure a support system.

1. Teachers, teammates, friends, coaches, administrators, and even the janitors encouraged me daily as I pushed toward my goal.

They knew about my goal because I told them with my words and actions.

2. Count on your family and the power of prayer.

3. Find a study partner or a tutor for the toughest classes. This became the perfect practice for tough times at Notre Dame and at law school.

Hold on to change.

1. Be disciplined. That meant staying focused and staying out of trouble in situations where it would have been easy to give in. Each temptation you overcome, such as staying home to study and saying no to the party-going friends, serves to strengthen you.

2. Think and act like a champion. Be a team captain and gravitate toward other successful leaders who are committed to making and maintaining change. Respect others and the rules of law.

3. Rejoice in your successes. It's OK to have fun when the time is right. Then get ready for the next challenge.

Lou Holtz challenge: Told not to return for senior season in 1988, when the Irish won their last national championship.

Face up to change.

1. I had to accept that Coach Holtz had good reasons for wanting to push seniors out, but I couldn't allow that to happen with me. Was I really as good as I thought I was?

2. My plans to get a graduate degree during fifth year at Notre Dame would be derailed. I didn't have the money to get that

degree unless I was on a scholarship. This was a life-changing situation.

3. This was just another challenge: I would have to commit everything to staying with the Irish and being a champion.

Learn your capacity to change.

1. Every challenge I'd overcome prepared me to make this change. Do I have the ability to be the best? I had to question, Can I deliver on what he is asking?

2. This was happening as I was finishing my bachelor's degree, so I had to resolve to not let up in my academic pursuits either. Could I handle the rigors of grad school while competing with so many changes with the team? The linebacking coach was new. I had to prove to him again that I was a starter.

3. There are times when you have to ask yourself that I don't have the capacity to succeed, thus your options become "Shall I quit or moan?" That's so often what people do—moan. I learned more than anything that I never quit.

Adopt a plan of action.

1. First, I had to convince Coach Holtz to let me stay on the team. I had to do this with respect and speed. I called him relentlessly until he met with me again and laid out my position.

2. I accepted his demands that I was on a short leash. I simply couldn't screw up in any way, or I was gone.

3. Consistent excellence was mandatory. I decided to be the first player in the weight room and last off the field. I would go all out whenever I was on the field, whether it was in practice or in scrimmages. I vowed to draw notice as the most unstoppable

linebacker on the field and the strongest team member in the weight room.

Secure a support system.

1. I started hanging out with the hardest-working players on the Irish—the ones who were focused on being champions. It would take great camaraderie, great discipline, and great talent to win a title. We had them.

2. I never missed a workout and always pushed to get stronger. This drew the notice of all the coaches who would make the decisions about my playing time.

3. I made sure I kept up with my classes. One way I did so was constantly communicating with the graduate professors. These guys have high expectations about academics. They supported me because they knew I worked hard and I cared about education. You have to walk a huge balancing act to achieve in both arenas.

Hold on to change.

1. I had the best spring game of my career and never let up through the summer and preseason.

2. I entered the season as a starter, and we went on to win the national championship.

3. Still, I faced another disappointment when my playing time was reduced midway through the season. I respectfully talked to Coach Holtz and laid out my case why that was unfair and why I deserved more playing time. He agreed after consulting with assistant coaches, and I started playing a lot more.

Wernle challenge: Residential treatment facility was floundering when I was hired in 2001. Today, it's considered a leader in its field.

Face up to change.

1. Change was essential to survival: Wernle was more than 120 years old and struggling month to month when I came here in 2001.

2. We were fourteen children under census. That's a loss of about $1 million a year. Wernle was in danger of losing its state certifications.

3. We had no savings, no strategic plan for the future, and low statewide rankings.

Learn your capacity to change.

1. We assessed where we were and whether we had the resources to move forward. We could reach excellence, but it would take time.

2. I had to determine whether our current board and executive staff could make the needed changes. Were they committed to building a solid program—one that was well respected in the community, the state, and around the nation for having great outcomes with abused and abandoned children?

3. Many of Wernle's issues dealt with image. We needed to sell ourselves better with marketing and with results, then constantly keep improving. You have to earn respect.

Adopt a plan of action.

1. We decided to make some quick and drastic changes. The only way to deal with huge problems is to change the culture and the mind-set of people.

2. We hired a completely new executive staff that would embrace a new vision and mission for Wernle. At the same time, the board also did its diligence in evaluating individual commitments and relevance.

3. We started developing strategic plans even as we worked to solve the immediate problems.

Secure a support system.

1. The board and staff became committed to embracing change. Those were imperative to our consistent improvement. The board would prod us and challenge us to perform better. We work constantly on team building.

2. The heart of nonprofits is fund-raising. We worked to build a network of people who could share in our vision and could help us financially.

3. We worked to improve relations with state agencies that determine the flow of young men into our residential treatment center. Then we had to prove that we could clinically treat children better than anywhere else.

Hold on to change.

1. Every employee knows their expectations and their parts in the mission. They are focused on positive results in treating and educating our children. Our state-leading statistics and national accreditation prove our successes.

2. Wernle is now a ten-million-a-year business that is an economic engine in the area. Our employment is surging, and pay is rising. We create dozens of heartwarming success stories each year. We run strategically while realizing our business is in a constantly shifting environment.

3. We are a campus of change. It's mandatory for us to constantly grow as we navigate a changing environment of governmental cutbacks and changes in priorities. We have successfully completed a $10 million campaign to replace buildings and institute new programs that will help us reach young people for another century.

CHAPTER 18

Nephew and FLASH

I DON'T HAVE TO go any farther than my dad's dining room table to illustrate that FLASH points can help overcome major obstacles. My dad, Chris, and I helped my nephew Rahfeal go back to college by devising five-step plans to support him. We met for several hours on a cold Sunday night several years ago to put a strategic plan into play that would use every one of the FLASH points.

Rahfeal is a charismatic young man with big ideas who hit the wall in finishing his undergraduate degree at Montclair State University in eastern New Jersey. My dad, Chris, and I convened the gathering because Rahfeal had reached out to us. His father—my oldest brother, Cedric—also had asked us to help. So had other caring aunts and uncles who were aware of the situation.

Let me step back now and explain why that is so important. Rahfeal and his three brothers experienced a different childhood than I. Chris and I were going to college and starting our careers, so we didn't know where they were at times after their mother got custody of them. We came to find out that they sometimes could not be found. They shuttled between family members to help support the process.

They were neglected and abandoned at points in their lives, much like the young men who need the services of Wernle Youth & Family Treatment Center. Those circumstances often lead to extremely negative development issues.

We knew Rahfeal displayed attention deficit issues, yet he was highly social and intelligent. It's simply amazing that he came out of that early environment to make it through high school and much of college. One of his younger brothers was shot dead in a gang-related incident. My aunts and uncles deserve great credit for reaching out and offering love and support for them.

I wish now that I was able to help out earlier. But that wasn't possible. We could have attempted to help much earlier and failed miserably because I didn't have the experience or the resources to help at that time.

It's hard for some people in need to understand, but you have to focus first on you and your immediate family. You will be prepared to help someone more if you are settled and strong. We now collectively had a breadth of experiences to develop strategies to help in these kinds of situations. We had the resources to help.

Rahfeal had fallen twenty-two hours short of finishing his degree in marketing. That fact burned at him for years. He is engaging and bright and has very high success potential. Put him in a room, and he lights it up. Recently, I accompanied him through the library and another government building on a rainy afternoon in Hillside, New Jersey. We could hardly move through the halls without a hug or a high-five from friends and acquaintances.

The future Rahfeal envisioned—as a successful businessman and entertainment entrepreneur—would be enhanced with a college degree. It would open doors and ignite his confidence. My dad, Chris, and I were absolutely certain that positive things would happen for Rahfeal if we could help guide him toward graduation.

He had a lot of positives going, anyway. He had earned good grades in his classes and had been involved on campus. He had already written a short heartfelt book about his tough life while growing up. He's a master at motivational speaking and setting up events. In fact, he's set up many events in the United States and even overseas.

We were confident at that meeting around the dinner table that we could set a graduation plan in motion and deflect the hurdles that Rahfeal would face. He could count on us for advice and financial support. Dad, Chris, and I invested $3,500 each. We expected Rahfeal to do the hard work. When it comes to getting the job done, support certainly helps. But we all believe that coddling doesn't help at all.

Our family histories and career successes had proven to us that the high majority of serious changes require commitment as well as a support system of caring people. Those serious changes often require a complete shift in lifestyle and environment. Rahfeal certainly needed to make serious changes.

His future was so important to us that we all had made major commitments before we reached the dinner table. Chris flew in from California, and I flew from Indiana to reach my dad's house near Newark.

A critical aspect of the team approach was for Rahfeal to be committed to the goal and follow through on the plan. We decided to convene the meeting with Rahfeal as we would to solve any business or personal problem. We all listened and asked questions. Our decisions and plans were reached by consensus. Rahfeal obviously needed some moral support, but we also found out that he needed some money to pay previous college debts.

He also needed a boost of motivation. He had mentioned through the years that he had looked up to Chris and me for getting our degrees and forging strong professional careers. He had seen both of us do internships on Wall Street.

There were times that Rahfeal and I would talk for hours about personal and spiritual growth. One time, we chatted in a car for several hours. Other times, we talked long into the night via cell phone. I always talked about commitment and getting into a position to succeed. Classwork was far harder for me than anything I did on the football field (except maybe three-a-day practices and alarm clocks going off at 4:30 AM).

I often advised him that perfecting a craft is the hardest part. For example, being a speaker is far more than marketing yourself. You have to practice and perfect your performance technique.

By the way, humor is a definite part of communications and goals. Life has to be fun too. It doesn't hurt to bring in some levity and self-deprecation into serious conversations. People like Rahfeal who want to make serious changes are already beating themselves up, so piling on the negatives isn't productive.

It certainly helped me at Notre Dame that I couldn't slack off without losing football eligibility. It was an ironclad rule for Irish players that we keep up with our classes and earn passing grades. All recruits are told that they are expected to graduate on time. There really was no option about taking a year or two off. There was no room for doubts to creep in.

Dad is savvy, friendly, and fair, but he is also very firm about people finishing the tasks that they start. I remember clearly that he—and my mom too—registered severe displeasure when I received a probation notice at Notre Dame. Dad didn't just let me know his disappointment with his words. He also said no to providing me with a car when I was back home from school. I had to catch rides with him or take the bus. He wanted me to earn the good things in life.

There comes a point in many lives when major changes aren't possible without help. Rahfeal had reached that point.

Deciding to make a monumental change is one thing. Navigating toward success is another. Failure usually happens in the great in-between time. That's when help is most often needed the most.

Let me show you an example: I often close my motivational speeches by asking for a volunteer to walk across a rope that is stretched along the floor. The goal of the exercise is to finish an imaginary change by the time the volunteer crosses it. That's simple enough. Most stumble off the rope a few times but laugh as they finish (always to applause from the audience). They have accomplished their goal.

I then make the challenge more difficult. I ask the volunteer to imagine there is a 300-foot drop below the rope. Would they attempt to walk across then? The obvious answer is no. There could be no stumbles this time. One slip would mean certain death. But next I ask them if they would reconsider if two or three people surrounded them and held them up as they all crossed together. The answer is always yes.

The point is, we all need support to make the major changes and to cross the major valleys in life.

The three of us played different roles as we helped Rahfeal focus on his goal.

Chris was the operational guy. He did much of the talking at the meeting. For one, he is closest in age, and he is very empathetic. He was the one who said, "Do this, and you can graduate in six months."

I was more the strategist and visionary. I wanted Rahfeal to envision himself with a degree. That's what I do with my daughter and son. Even though they are young, I don't want them to ever question the value of education. I want them to be immersed in education and in the college experience from an early age.

My dad offered a mix of encouragement and "get it done" focus. We devised a four-month plan that required class attendance mixed with online classes.

Rahfeal worked hard to make it happen and quickly made up the twenty-two hours. But he hit the wall again with a foreign language requirement. He just didn't believe he could pass the Italian class and wanted to put it off. We implored him to keep going and do anything to pass that course with a C average. That was a profound moment.

That's when support was needed the most. "Get in there and finish it," we pushed. It really came down to the old Nike slogan: "Just do it!"

Rahfeal finally did it. He got a C and passed the Italian class.

Now let's summarize Rahfeal's direction through FLASH points:

Face up to change.

We knew that Rahfeal was ready to act from the tone of our conversations in person and via phone and email. He had decided enough was enough. He came to us. That's important. We were motivated into action because Rahfeal finally said he wasn't satisfied with his position in life and his frustrations. He said that it was time to stop talking and to start acting on getting his degree.

When he had proved that he was ready to put in the time and work it would take to achieve his goal, we were motivated into action.

Learn your capacity to change.

We knew going into the meeting that Rahfeal had the capacity to change. He had already proven he could pass classes and succeed in a collegiate environment. It became more of a motivation to shed the barriers. We focused on presenting him with some of the tools he needed.

Adopt a plan of action.

The goal was simple going into our family meeting to help Rahfeal: to create an operational plan that would surround him and prop him up as he finished his degree. We devised a one-semester plan that mixed class attendance, along with online classes for twenty-two hours. We worked to figure out the financial needs and agreed on our parts in it. We made sure the plan was followed.

Secure a support system.

It was imperative that Rahfeal reach out for the guidance and that he was part of devising the plan. He would have to do the work, and it wouldn't be easy, but we were there to catch him if it appeared he would fall. We stressed having a support system outside of the three of us. Rahfeal needed to enlist his teachers, his friends, and his family in his change. They all would play a role. The teachers would have to know that he was serious about learning. His friends and family would have to know that his changes might affect their times together. His social life had to take a back seat. This was truly a shared sacrifice.

Hold on to change.

The plan worked. We all attended Rahfeal's graduation with smiles on our faces. There were lots of tears too. Rahfeal had made one of the biggest changes in his life to relieve a burden and accomplish a life goal. Now he works in marketing for the entertainment industry and travels the country and the world. He can forever boast that he is a college graduate.

He has relieved a burden on his life and now is focused forward. He wants more.

Those who desire major changes must have the ability to focus on their goals. They have to find a way to commit themselves and keep working on them. The *graduated* note on your college transcript tells future employers that you can finish multiple tasks, that you are well-rounded, and that you can follow through on assignments.

I earned my undergraduate degree from Notre Dame, and Chris earned his from Brown at a four-year, on-time pace. Recent national figures publicized by *U.S. News and World Report* magazine show that 90 percent of students graduate on time at Notre Dame—fourth best for all universities—and 86 percent graduate on time at Brown.

We were amazingly fortunate to get into schools that push their students and offer such results. Finishing college in four years is the best way to do it, I think, but certainly not the only way. In fact, only 60 percent of students graduate within six years, according to a 2008 report by the National Center for Higher Education Management Systems. And the national average is less than 50 percent for African American males.

You can't change a person's upbringing, but you can help change his or her current state. You have to take ownership of your shortcomings no matter why you have them.

The fun things in life must be pushed aside for a while sometimes in order to gain success. Enjoy the things you love, but don't allow them to be barriers.

CONCLUSION

NOW THAT YOU have learned about the trials and tribulations I have overcome in my life, I hope my story of perseverance will inspire you to dream big in your own life and never give up on reaching your goals.

But first, you have to make the critical decision to change. It sounds easy, but it's really very complex. Studies show there is a big gap between how people perceive themselves and how they really are when it comes to being proactive about change. That fact is always illuminated in my presentations when I ask audience members to indicate what kind of "get it done" personality they have. I give them three options:

Are you someone who makes things happen?

Are you someone who watches things happen?

Or are you someone who often finds yourself asking, What just happened?

The third question always draws laughs and some humorous finger-pointing.

Approximately 75 percent of people tell me they see themselves as doers and assure me that they *definitely* make things happen. However, studies have shown that only 20 percent of people actually make things happen. That means 55 percent of people are just fooling themselves. There's a very big disconnect between how people see themselves and how they really are.

Statistics show that 60 percent play a passive role in change. They are observers of the game rather than players in it. They envy those who've made serious changes, but they are more likely to talk about making a change than doing so.

One thing that pops up time and again in my roles as CEO, friend, father, author, and motivational speaker is that people who are willing to change are willing to listen. You can't learn while talking. So listen up and take notes.

You won't change by maintaining the status quo—doing it the same as you've always done at home, on the job, or anywhere. Ever heard the old saying "Insanity is doing the same thing over and over and expecting different results"? It's true. If you want your life to change, *you* have to change. And my FLASH points are your roadmap for how to do that. I believe in you. Now it's time to believe in yourself.

HOW TO CHANGE USING FLASH POINTS

Face up to change.

1. ______________________________
2. ______________________________
3. ______________________________

Learn your capacity to change.

1. ______________________________
2. ______________________________
3. ______________________________

Adopt a plan of action.

1. ______________________________
2. ______________________________
3. ______________________________

Secure a support system.

1. ______________________________
2. ______________________________
3. ______________________________

Hold on to change.

1. ______________________________
2. ______________________________
3. ______________________________

Printed in the United States
By Bookmasters